one
pot

one pot

OVER 100 DELICIOUS RECIPES

hamlyn

First published in Great Britain in 2005 by
Hamlyn, a division of Octopus Publishing Group Ltd
2–4 Heron Quays, London E14 4JP

This edition published 2007 for Index Books Ltd

Copyright © Octopus Publishing Group Ltd 2005

ISBN-13: 978-0-600-61696-2
ISBN-10: 0-600-61696-7

A CIP catalogue record for this book is available from the British Library.

Printed and bound in China

10 9 8 7 6 5 4 3 2 1

Notes

Standard level spoon measures are used in all recipes
1 tablespoon = one 15 ml spoon
1 teaspoon = one 5 ml spoon

Both metric and imperial measurements are given for the recipes. Use one set of measurements only, not a mixture of both.

Ovens should be preheated to the specified temperature. If using a fan-assisted oven, follow the manufacturer's instructions for adjusting the time and temperature.

This book includes dishes made with nuts and nut derivatives. It is advisable for those with known allergic reactions to nuts and nut derivatives and those who may be potentially vulnerable to these allergies, such as pregnant and nursing mothers, invalids, the elderly, babies and children, to avoid dishes made with nuts and nut oils. It is also prudent to check the labels of preprepared ingredients for the possible inclusion of nut derivatives.

Medium eggs have been used throughout.

The Department of Health advises that eggs should not be consumed raw. This book contains some dishes made with raw or lightly cooked eggs. It is prudent for more vulnerable people such as pregnant and nursing mothers, invalids, the elderly, babies and young children to avoid uncooked or lightly cooked dishes made with eggs.

Meat and poultry should be cooked thoroughly. To test if poultry is cooked, pierce the flesh through the thickest part with a skewer or fork – the juices should run clear, never pink or red.

contents

introduction   6

crowd-pleasing casseroles   14

simply soups   50

international inspiration   72

vegetable heaven   104

beans, rice, grains   122

index   142
acknowledgements   144

introduction

From the moment when our distant ancestors learnt how to rub two sticks together to make a fire, people have enjoyed the benefits of one-pot cooking. This simple yet wonderfully versatile method essentially involves preparing and cooking your meal in one pot or dish. However, far from limiting the type of recipes or food that can be prepared, one-pot cooking is actually extremely diverse. There are endless possibilities from soups and casseroles to stir-fries and curries and, with 100 recipes to choose from here, you may find yourself being completely converted to the one-pot method. The pot itself may be a large frying pan, saucepan, a casserole or a stainless steel pan which can fit a steamer neatly on top for cooking vegetables or couscous. It all depends on the recipe but, apart from the occasional bit of extra preparation, everything will be cooked in and served from just one pot.

EASY DOES IT

One-pot cooking is the ideal solution for anyone with a busy lifestyle: whether you're a student, a full-time mum or a working parent, time will probably be a precious commodity. While it's always lovely to sit down and enjoy a home-cooked meal, the thought of preparing and cooking various different ingredients on the stove and in the oven, then assembling the finished dish, can often make it seem a bit too much like hard work after a hectic day. Add to this the washing up and clearing away afterwards, and a takeaway or quick snack will often be more appealing. However, with one-pot cooking most of the hassle factor is removed as those piles of dirty dishes, pans and utensils are reduced to a manageable amount while most of the preparation, and quite often the cooking, can be done in advance, so you can just relax and enjoy the meal without all the hard work.

A HEALTHY OPTION

Nowadays everyone is more aware of the benefits of eating a well-balanced diet and one-pot cooking is a healthy method of cooking for a number of reasons, not least the inclusion of all those lovely fresh ingredients. When you use a steamer to cook vegetables, most of the vitamins and minerals are retained, rather than being washed down the sink, as they are when you drain away the cooking water from boiled vegetables. As one-pot cooking can involve a lot of steaming, you know that you're getting the real benefits from your

Cooking a heart-warming stew in one pot is an easy way of creating an informal dinner with minimum fuss.

fresh ingredients. Also, with many soups and stews, the vegetables are cooked in the actual dish, again retaining all of that goodness. One-pot cooking also features lots of warming casseroles, many of which include beans, pulses and grains, which are all extremely beneficial to our diet, providing plenty of protein and fibre.

ECONOMICAL COOKING

One-pot cooking is also a very economical way to prepare food. Soups in particular are a great way of using up odd vegetables that you have leftover from other meals, while stews and casseroles can use meat in the same way. Also, if you're just cooking for one or two people, you can freeze any of the meal that you don't use, and you have another meal, ready to simply reheat when you need to – so it's economical in terms of money and time! In fact, it often makes sense to cook in bulk anyway; with one big cooking session in the kitchen you can have a series of meals prepared for the week ahead.

SOMETHING FOR EVERYONE

While soups, stews and casseroles are undoubtedly a big feature of one-pot cooking, they are by no means exclusive. There are so many different meals that can be prepared this way that every taste is catered for and there are plenty of options for vegetarians too, with recipes such as *Quick Thai Vegetable Curry* (see page 112) and *Chestnut Sofrito* (see page 109). Using a stainless steel pot and steamer means that you can make virtually any type of meal in one go, as rice, vegetables and couscous can be steaming away while the rest of your meal cooks underneath.

FLAVOURS OF THE WORLD

If we look at cuisines from around the world, we can see that one-pot cooking features quite heavily. From Italian

One-pot cooking helps to preserve all the goodness present in fresh vegetables.

risottos to Moroccan tagines, this method of preparing food has remained an invaluable cooking technique because it's so practical; wonderful, flavoursome food can be created with a minimum of fuss and the most basic of equipment and facilities. *Thai Monkfish and Prawn Curry* (see page 98), *Cambodian Fish Hotpot* (page 48), and *Moroccan Red Chicken* (see page 76) are just a few of the gorgeous global recipes that you can enjoy, along with classics such as *Coq au Vin* (see page 84) and *Irish Stew* (see page 31).

One-pot cooking lends itself perfectly to experimenting with new flavours and ingredients because the recipes are so easy to follow and the cooking instructions so simple, that it's difficult to go too far wrong. So, if you wouldn't describe yourself as a particularly experienced chef then this is a great place to gain some confidence with new dishes. If you are handy in the kitchen, however, then here's your opportunity to take things easy while still impressing family and friends.

EQUIPMENT

Pot and steamer

Your most essential piece of equipment is the pot. A special one-pot set, comprising a large stainless steel pan with a tight-fitting removable steamer and lid, should cover all eventualities. However, this is by no means the only option and alternatives include a large, heavy-based saucepan and a vegetable steamer that can be balanced on top or, for oven-cooked recipes, a large, ovenproof casserole with a lid will be more than adequate.

Heavy-based frying pan

In a few of the recipes, there will be an initial browning or frying of some ingredients. This is often best done in a separate, heavy-based frying pan before removing the ingredients to the cooking pot.

Slotted spoon and large serving spoon

A slotted spoon is useful for removing larger ingredients to serving plates, for example, when transferring pieces of cooked chicken or other meat, before you spoon the sauce over the top. A large serving spoon will be necessary for serving stews and soups.

Measuring spoons

You'll need these for measuring out spices, oil and other smaller amounts of ingredients.

Oven gloves

As one-pot cooking often involves removing the pot from the hob to the oven and out again to serve, oven gloves are a really important piece of equipment.

Heatproof mat

This is essential for when you're serving from the cooking pot, as you'll want to put it on the table but

A pot-and-steamer set is a worthwhile investment as it will allow you to cook all your ingredients at the same time.

avoid the risk of burn marks. Warming winter soups and casseroles are always best served from the pot, as the contents will be kept nice and hot for longer, should anyone want a second serving!

INGREDIENTS

Stock

Stock is a key ingredient for many of the recipes in this book. It's particularly important to have a really good quality stock for soups and risottos as it will have a big impact on the flavour of the finished dish. A homemade stock is definitely worth the effort and, although it will take a little while to prepare, it's very easy and can just be left bubbling away on its own. You'll find recipes for chicken, vegetable, beef and fish stocks on pages 10–13, so when you have a little time to spare, make a big batch and freeze it to use in future recipes.

Spices

There are certain spices that you'll see appearing in many recipes, particularly in Asian and Moroccan dishes, so it's good to have an assortment in your store-cupboard. Coriander, saffron, cumin, cloves and cinnamon are some of the most commonly used spices and different combinations will produce a real variety of flavours.

Herbs

Sage, rosemary, mint, parsley and basil are just some of the herbs that you'll need for the recipes in this book. If you have a choice, always go for fresh herbs, as the flavour is so much better. Dried herbs will suffice if you can't get hold of fresh, but remember to halve the quantities. Another option is to use frozen herbs and you can either freeze your own or, alternatively, some varieties are available in supermarkets.

Olive oil

As a general rule, extra virgin olive oil is the best-quality, as it comes from the first pressing of the olives, followed by virgin olive oil and finally, regular olive oil will be the

Fill your store-cupboard with an assortment of spices so that they're always close at hand.

lowest quality. You will need to judge for yourself which oil to use, however, if a recipe specifies using extra virgin, it's obviously important for the flavour of the dish – as with risottos – so you should follow the advice.

Olives

A lot of North African dishes include olives and although we don't have anywhere near the choice of olives here as are available in countries such as Morocco, try to get as close as you can to the type listed in the ingredients of the recipe. As with olive oil, different types of olive will have an impact on the flavour of the recipe.

FRESH IS BEST

It goes without saying that the fresher the vegetables you use, the better. This applies not only to taste, but to health benefits too, as really fresh produce will have the highest vitamin content. Always buy the best quality you can afford as you'll really notice the difference in the finished dish. Look out for nice plump tomatoes (choose sun-ripened or vine tomatoes for even greater flavour), bright broccoli and greens, and firm carrots and potatoes.

Use fresh herbs to add depth of flavour to any dish. Add delicate leafy herbs toward the end of cooking so they are not burned.

stock

chicken stock

MAKES ABOUT 2.5 LITRES/4 PINTS

1.3 kg/3 lb chicken wings and necks
2 onions, cut into wedges
4 litres/7 pints water
2 carrots, chopped
2 celery sticks, chopped
10 parsley sprigs
2 thyme sprigs
2 bay leaves
10 black peppercorns

Put the chicken wings and necks and the onions in a large heavy-based saucepan. Cook over a low heat, stirring frequently, until lightly browned all over.

Add the water and bring to the boil, scraping up any sediment from the bottom of the pan with a wooden spoon. Skim off the scum that rises to the surface. Add the carrots, celery, parsley, thyme, bay leaves and peppercorns, then partially cover the pan and simmer gently for 3 hours.

Remove the pan from the heat and strain the stock. Cover the stock and leave to cool, then chill in the refrigerator overnight. Remove and discard the layer of fat that will have set on the surface. Store in the refrigerator until required or freeze.

vegetable stock

MAKES ABOUT 600 ML/1 PINT

50 g/2 oz butter

2 onions, chopped

2 leeks, thinly sliced

2 carrots, chopped

2 celery sticks, chopped

1 fennel bulb, chopped

1 thyme sprig

1 marjoram sprig

1 fennel sprig

4 parsley sprigs

900 ml/1½ pints water

Melt the butter in a large heavy-based saucepan. Add the onions, leeks, carrots, celery and fennel, stir well to coat, then cover and cook over a low heat for 10 minutes.

Stir in the thyme, marjoram, fennel and parsley and add the water. Bring to the boil, then cover the pan and simmer for 15 minutes.

Remove the pan from the heat and strain the stock. Cover and leave to cool, then store in the refrigerator until required or freeze.

beef stock

MAKES ABOUT 2 LITRES/3½ PINTS

1.75 kg/3½ lb beef bones, chopped into
    7 cm/3 inch pieces

2 onions, quartered

2 carrots, chopped

2 celery sticks, chopped

2 tomatoes, chopped

4 litres/7 pints water

10 parsley sprigs

4 thyme sprigs

2 bay leaves

8 black peppercorns

Put the beef bones into a large roasting tin and roast in a preheated oven, 230°C (450°F), Gas Mark 8, for 30 minutes, until lightly browned and the fat and juices run out. Turn the bones occasionally during cooking. Add the onions, carrots, celery and tomatoes, spoon over the fat in the tin and roast, stirring occasionally, for a further 30 minutes.

Using a slotted spoon, transfer the bones and vegetables to a large saucepan. Pour off the fat from the roasting tin and add 150 ml/¼ pint of the water. Set the roasting tin over a low heat and bring to the boil, scraping up any sediment from the base of the pan. Pour this into the saucepan and add the remaining water.

Bring to the boil, skimming off the scum that rises to the surface. Add the parsley, thyme, bay leaves and peppercorns. Partially cover the pan, then lower the heat and simmer for 4 hours.

Strain the stock, cover and leave to cool. Chill in the refrigerator overnight, then remove and discard the layer of fat that will have set on the surface.

fish stock

MAKES ABOUT 1 LITRE/1¾ PINTS

25 g/1 oz butter

3 shallots, roughly chopped

1 small leek, roughly chopped

1 celery stick or piece of fennel, roughly
   chopped

1 kg/2 lb white fish or shellfish bones,
   heads and trimmings

150 ml/¼ pint dry white wine

several parsley stalks

½ lemon, sliced

1 teaspoon black or white peppercorns

1 litre/1¾ pints cold water

Melt the butter in a large heavy-based saucepan until bubbling.
Add all the vegetables and fry gently for 5 minutes to soften them slightly,
without browning. Add the fish bones, wine, parsley, lemon slices,
peppercorns and cold water.

Bring to the boil, skimming off the scum that rises to the surface.
Reduce the heat and simmer the stock for 20 minutes.

Strain the stock, cover and leave to cool. Chill in the refrigerator
overnight, then remove and discard the layer of fat that will have set on
the surface.

chicken with lemon and olives

This is a speedy variation of the traditional Moroccan recipe for chicken with lemons and olives, making it relevant to modern cooking.

SERVES 2

6 small or 4 large chicken thighs

2 large garlic cloves

2 teaspoons ground cumin

2 teaspoons paprika

4 tablespoons olive oil

1 onion, finely chopped

1 teaspoon saffron threads

juice of 1 large lemon

250 ml/8 fl oz Chicken Stock
   (see page 10)

1 large lemon, sliced

125 g/4 oz green olives, pitted

salt and pepper

Put the chicken thighs into a dish. Crush the garlic with a pinch of salt, the cumin, paprika and plenty of black pepper. Blend with half of the oil, then spoon over the chicken and stir well to mix thoroughly. Cover and leave in a cool place to marinate for up to 4 hours.

Heat the remaining oil in a small, shallow, flameproof cassserole, add the chicken and brown evenly. Remove with a slotted spoon and drain on kitchen paper.

Add the onion to the pan and fry, stirring occasionally, until soft and golden. Stir in the saffron and cook for 1 minute, then return the chicken to the pan. Pour over the lemon juice and stock. Add the sliced lemon and heat to simmering point. Add the olives, cover the pan and adjust the heat so the liquid gives an occasional bubble. Cook for about 15–20 minutes, turning the chicken thighs two or three times, until they are tender. If necessary, remove the chicken to a warmed serving platter and boil the cooking juices hard until reduced to a thick sauce. Spoon the sauce over the chicken.

easy one-pot chicken

As the title suggests, this is an easy dish – perfect for when you want a hearty meal without a lot of effort.

SERVES 2

1 kg/2 lb chicken

1 onion, quartered

3 carrots, about 200 g/7 oz, quartered

2 medium baking potatoes, about 325 g/11 oz, quartered

½ lemon, sliced

bunch of fresh mixed herbs or a dried bouquet garni

750 ml/1¼ pints Chicken Stock (see page 10)

2 teaspoons Dijon mustard

15 g/½ oz butter

a little paprika

125 g/4 oz broccoli, cut into florets

salt and pepper

Put the chicken, breast-side down, into a medium flameproof casserole. Arrange the onion, carrots and potatoes around the chicken and add the lemon slices and herbs. Mix the stock with the mustard and pour into the casserole. Season with salt and pepper and bring to the boil.

Cover the casserole and transfer to a preheated oven, 180°C (350°F), Gas Mark 4, for 1 hour, or until the chicken juices run clear when a skewer is inserted into the thickest part of the leg and breast.

Turn the chicken over. Dot the butter over the breast and legs and sprinkle with paprika. Tuck the broccoli florets around the chicken, pressing them below the level of the stock. Return the casserole to the oven and cook uncovered for 15 minutes, or until the chicken is golden and the broccoli is tender.

Carve the chicken and arrange in shallow soup bowls with the vegetables and stock.

FOOD **FACT**
Broccoli is packed full of essential nutrients such as vitamin C and fibre. It's a perfect vegetable for one-pot recipes as all the goodness stays in the finished dish.

roasted duck
with spiced lentils

This is more of a one-dish roast than a one-pot stew, but nevertheless it is simple to prepare and cook. Duck works well with the rustic flavours of the Puy lentils and red cabbage.

SERVES 2

175 g/6 oz red cabbage, finely shredded

100 g/3½ oz Puy lentils

1 dessert apple, cored and diced

1 small onion, chopped

6 ready-to-eat, dried, stoned prunes
    (optional)

300 ml/½ pint Chicken Stock
    (see page 10)

1 tablespoon wine vinegar

1 cinnamon stick, halved

4 cloves

2 duck legs, about 275 g/9 oz each

salt and pepper

thyme, to garnish (optional)

Put the cabbage, lentils, apple, onion and prunes, if using, into a shallow ovenproof dish or roasting tin. Pour over the stock, then add the vinegar, cinnamon and cloves and season with salt and pepper to taste.

Arrange the duck legs on a roasting rack and place it over the dish or roasting tin. Prick the duck skin with a small knife or skewer and sprinkle with salt.

Roast the duck in a preheated oven, 200°C (400°F), Gas Mark 6, for 45 minutes, or until the skin is crispy and the cabbage and lentils are tender. Spoon on to plates, discarding the cinnamon and cloves and serve.

spicy duck in port
with fresh figs

A real winter warmer, prepare this dish when you're entertaining. Try and marinate the duck overnight, if possible, as the flavours will be more intense.

Place the duck in a large bowl, add all the marinade ingredients and stir well. Cover and leave in the refrigerator to marinate for at least 2 hours or overnight.

Remove the duck from the marinade, reserving the marinade, and pat dry. Heat a large flameproof casserole over a moderate heat, add the duck, a few pieces at a time, skin-side down first, and brown well all over. Transfer each batch to a colander to drain. Pour off most of the fat, leaving about 1 tablespoon.

Add the onion and garlic to the casserole and cook gently for 5 minutes until softened. Return the duck pieces and pour in the marinade. Bring to the boil and add the stock. Bring back to the boil, reduce the heat and season with salt and pepper. Cover with a tight-fitting lid and simmer gently for 45 minutes.

Remove the lid, skim off any fat and place the figs on top. Cover and cook for 20–30 minutes until the duck and figs are tender.

Remove the duck and figs from the casserole and keep warm. Remove the star anise, cinnamon, bay leaf and thyme. Skim off as much fat as possible. Increase the heat and boil rapidly until the sauce is reduced by half. Serve the duck with the sauce.

SERVES 4

2 kg/4 lb duck, cut into 8 pieces

1 onion, chopped

1–2 garlic cloves, crushed

500 ml/17 fl oz Chicken Stock (see page 10) or veal stock

12 ripe figs

salt and pepper

MARINADE

400 ml/14 fl oz port

4 whole star anise

5 cm/2 inch piece of cinnamon stick

4 cloves

8 Szechuan or black peppercorns

2 tablespoons chopped stem ginger

4 tablespoons clear honey

1 piece of dried or fresh orange or tangerine peel

1 bay leaf

1 thyme sprig

braised pheasant with marsala
and chestnuts

The pheasant and chestnuts make this a real festive meal but, if you can find the ingredients, you should try this recipe any time of the year.

SERVES 4

500 g/1 lb fresh chestnuts or 250 g/8 oz
  vacuum-packed cooked chestnuts

25 g/1 oz butter

1 pheasant, about 1–1.25 kg/2–2½ lb

125 g/4 oz pancetta or streaky bacon,
  cut into strips

1 large onion, chopped

1 celery stick, chopped

1 large carrot, chopped

1 tablespoon chopped sage

125 ml/4 fl oz Marsala

500 ml/17 fl oz Chicken Stock
  (see page 10) or game stock

salt and pepper

If using fresh chestnuts, cut a slash in the pointed end of each one. Place the chestnuts in a saucepan and cover with water, then bring to the boil and simmer for 2 minutes. Remove the pan from the heat. Using a slotted spoon, take out one chestnut at a time and remove the outer and inner skins. If the skins are difficult to peel, return the pan to the heat, bring back to the boil and repeat the process.

Melt the butter in a large flameproof casserole over a moderate heat, brown the pheasant all over, then transfer the bird to a plate. Reduce the heat, add the pancetta or bacon and cook for 1 minute. Add the onion, celery and carrot and cook until the onion has softened.

Return the pheasant to the casserole and add the sage, Marsala, stock, and the chestnuts, if using fresh ones. Season with salt and pepper and bring to the boil. Cover with a tight-fitting lid and simmer gently for 35–45 minutes until the pheasant and chestnuts are cooked. Alternatively, cook in a preheated oven, 160°C (325°F), Gas Mark 3. If using vacuum-packed chestnuts, add them after 20–25 minutes.

Remove the pheasant from the casserole and keep it warm. Skim off any excess fat from the surface. Place the casserole over a moderate to high heat and boil rapidly until the sauce reduces and thickens slightly. Adjust the seasoning, then serve the pheasant with the sauce.

hunter-style rabbit stew

A simple peasant dish, said to be a favourite of Tuscan hunters, who would no doubt have skinned and barbecued their rabbit over a camp fire.

SERVES 4

1 rabbit, cut into 8 joints, reserving the liver

2 garlic cloves, crushed

1 tablespoon each chopped rosemary and sage

1 bottle dry red wine

2 tablespoons olive oil

500 g/1 lb ripe tomatoes, skinned, deseeded and chopped

2 tablespoons tomato purée

12 Tuscan black olives

salt and pepper

soft polenta or pappardelle noodles, to serve

Wash and dry the rabbit pieces and liver and place in a ceramic dish with the garlic, rosemary, sage, red wine and a plenty of salt and pepper. Cover and leave to marinate overnight.

Remove the rabbit pieces and the liver from the marinade and dry well on kitchen paper. Strain the marinade into a saucepan, bring to the boil and simmer until reduced by half, then strain through a fine sieve.

Heat the oil in a large flameproof casserole, add the rabbit and liver and brown on all sides. Add the reduced marinade, tomatoes and tomato purée. Bring to the boil and simmer gently, covered, for 1 hour, adding the olives for the final 15 minutes. Remove the rabbit to a warm plate, wrap loosely in foil and keep it warm.

Mash the liver into the sauce, then return the sauce to the boil and boil for 10 minutes until it is thick and glossy. Pour the sauce over the rabbit and serve with soft polenta or pappardelle noodles.

lamb and aubergine casserole
with a potato crust

It's important to salt and drain the aubergines so that you don't end up with too much extra liquid in the casserole.

SERVES 4

2 large aubergines, about 375 g/12 oz each

olive oil, for frying

1.5 kg/3 lb boneless leg or shoulder of lamb, cut into 3.5 cm/1½ inch cubes

1 onion, sliced

2 garlic cloves, crushed

500 g/1 lb fresh tomatoes, skinned and chopped, or 410 g/13½ oz can chopped tomatoes

1 tablespoon tomato purée

½ teaspoon ground allspice

1 teaspoon ground cumin

2 tablespoons rosemary leaves

75 ml/3 fl oz red wine vinegar

2 tablespoons sugar

salt and pepper

POTATO CRUST

500 g/1 lb potatoes

1 tablespoon chopped thyme

1 tablespoon chopped parsley

1 garlic clove, crushed

2 egg yolks

Slice the aubergines into 1 cm/½ inch rounds. Layer the slices in a colander set over a bowl, sprinkling each layer liberally with salt; set aside for 30 minutes.

Heat 2 tablespoons oil in a large flameproof casserole, and brown the lamb cubes well all over. Remove with a slotted spoon and set aside.

Add the onion and garlic to the casserole, with more oil if necessary, and cook gently for 5 minutes until softened. Add all the remaining ingredients except the aubergine and return the meat to the pan with any juices. Season with salt and pepper and bring to the boil, then cover and place in a preheated oven, 150°C (300°F), Gas Mark 2, for 1½ hours.

Rinse the aubergine slices thoroughly and pat dry. Heat some more oil in a large frying pan over a moderate heat and fry the aubergine slices lightly on both sides; do this in batches if necessary. Drain well and pat dry with kitchen paper.

To prepare the potato crust, coarsely grate the potatoes, then pat dry with kitchen paper. Stir in the thyme, parsley, garlic and egg yolks and season with salt and pepper.

Remove the casserole from the oven and skim off any fat from the surface. Stir in the aubergine slices and sprinkle over the potato mixture to cover. Increase the heat to 180°C (350°F), Gas Mark 4. Return the casserole to the oven, uncovered, for 30–35 minutes, or until the potato crust is lightly golden.

lamb with garlic, lemon
and mint

Sealing the meat first ensures that all the juices are locked inside which stops it from drying out when it cooks.

SERVES 4

3 tablespoons olive oil

1.5 kg/3 lb boneless leg or shoulder of lamb, trimmed and cut into 2.5–3.5 cm/1–1½ inch cubes

1 large onion, sliced

6 garlic cloves, crushed

1 tablespoon plain flour

3 tablespoons fresh lemon juice

large pinch of saffron threads

200 ml/7 fl oz dry white wine

3 tablespoons chopped mint

1 teaspoon finely grated lemon rind

salt and pepper

Heat the olive oil in a large flameproof casserole over a moderate heat, add the lamb cubes in batches and brown well all over. Remove with a slotted spoon and set aside.

Reduce the heat, add the onion and garlic and cook gently for 5–10 minutes until softened. Add the flour, stirring to blend it with the oil, then add the lemon juice, saffron and white wine. Stir in the lamb. Bring the wine to the boil, then reduce the heat, cover the casserole and cook for 1–1½ hours until the lamb is tender. Stir in the chopped mint and lemon rind and season to taste with salt and pepper.

lamb and lentil hotpot

In this simple hotpot, baking the lamb cutlets twice is what makes it deliciously succulent and tender.

SERVES 4

100 g/3½ oz green lentils, rinsed
8 lamb cutlets
2 tablespoons olive oil
2 onions, thinly sliced
2 garlic cloves, crushed
150 g/5 oz chestnut mushrooms, sliced
several rosemary sprigs
300 ml/½ pint Chicken Stock
    (see page 10) or lamb stock
875 g/1¾ lb potatoes
salt and pepper

Put the lentils into a small saucepan and cover with water. Bring to the boil and boil rapidly for 10 minutes. Drain and set aside.

Meanwhile, trim the lamb cutlets of any excess fat. Heat half the oil in a frying pan, add the cutlets and fry for 5 minutes, turning once, until browned. Arrange the cutlets in a shallow 1.8 litre/3 pint ovenproof dish.

Add the onions, garlic and mushrooms to the frying pan and fry for 3 minutes. Spoon over the cutlets. Add the lentils, rosemary, stock and a little salt and pepper to the frying pan and bring to the boil. Pour over the cutlets.

Thinly slice the potatoes and layer over the cutlets, seasoning the layers lightly with salt and pepper. Drizzle with the remaining oil. Bake in a preheated oven, 180°C (350°F), Gas Mark 4, for 45 minutes, or until the potatoes are turning pale golden. Leave to cool, then chill in the refrigerator for up to 24 hours.

To serve, bake in a preheated oven, 180°C (350°F), Gas Mark 4, for 45 minutes until golden.

irish stew

Cold weather and dark evenings put us in the mood for traditional, comforting hot food, such as this chunky meat and vegetable stew.

SERVES 4–5

750 g/1½ lb lean fillet or leg of lamb

1 tablespoon plain flour

2 tablespoons sunflower or vegetable oil

3 onions, cut into wedges

400 g/13 oz carrots, cut into chunks

875 g/1¾ lb potatoes, scrubbed and quartered

900 ml/1½ pints Chicken Stock (see page 10) or lamb stock

2 bay leaves

several thyme sprigs

2 tablespoons Worcestershire sauce

salt and pepper

Cut the lamb into even-sized cubes, discarding any excess fat. Season the flour with salt and pepper and coat the lamb.

Heat the oil in a large frying pan. Add the lamb and fry for 5–8 minutes until lightly browned. Remove the lamb with a slotted spoon and transfer to a large flameproof casserole. Add the onions and carrots to the frying pan and fry until lightly browned. Put into the casserole with the potatoes.

Add the stock, bay leaves, thyme and Worcestershire sauce to the pan and bring to the boil. Pour into the casserole and season lightly with salt and pepper. Cover and cook in a preheated oven, 180°C (350°F), Gas Mark 4, for 1 hour. Check the seasoning.

Leave the stew to cool, then chill in the refrigerator for up to 24 hours.

To serve, bring the stew almost to the boil, then reduce the heat, cover the casserole and simmer gently for 25 minutes, or until very hot.

FOOD FACT

The humble carrot is a great source of vitamin A. Instead of peeling your carrots, wash, then scrape them with the back of a knife, so you don't remove too much of the goodness that's contained in the outer layer.

paprika pork

This recipe bears similarities to the classic Hungarian Goulash, but the twist comes when it's time to serve – noodles instead of the usual rice.

SERVES 4

1–2 tablespoons olive oil

75 g/3 oz rindless streaky bacon, chopped

2 onions, chopped

2 garlic cloves, crushed

2 teaspoons paprika

250 g/8 oz tomatoes, skinned and chopped

1 tablespoon tomato purée

1.25 kg/2½ lb boneless shoulder of pork, trimmed and cut into 3.5 cm/1½ inch cubes

50 g/2 oz small pickled gherkins, cut into strips

1 tablespoon plain flour

75 ml/3 fl oz soured cream

salt and pepper

chopped parsley, to garnish

noodles, to serve

Heat 1 tablespoon of the oil in a large flameproof casserole over a moderate heat, add the bacon and cook for 1–2 minutes until it renders some fat. Reduce the heat and add the onions and garlic, adding more oil if necessary, and cook for 5–6 minutes until softened. Add the paprika and cook for 1–2 minutes.

Add the tomatoes, tomato purée and the pork to the casserole, with about 600 ml/1 pint water to cover. Season with salt and pepper and stir well. Bring to the boil, reduce the heat, cover the casserole and simmer gently for 1–1½ hours until the meat is tender.

When the meat is tender, stir the pickled gherkins into the casserole. In a small bowl, mix the flour with the soured cream to form a smooth paste. Stir thoroughly into the sauce and continue cooking for 10 minutes.

Sprinkle the stew with chopped parsley and serve with noodles.

pork and clam stew

Try to find small Venus or Palourde clams for this classic Portuguese dish;
the sweetness of the pork and the clams marry beautifully.

SERVES 4

2 tablespoons olive oil

1 kg/2 lb boneless pork loin, trimmed of excess fat, cut into 2.5 cm/1 inch cubes

1 large onion, chopped

2 garlic cloves, crushed

2 teaspoons paprika

250 ml/8 fl oz dry white wine, plus extra if needed

1 tablespoon white wine vinegar

1 bay leaf

3 red peppers, roasted, skinned, deseeded and cut into strips

1 kg/2 lb small clams, scrubbed well and rinsed, discarding any that stay open

15 g/½ oz chopped coriander leaves

salt and pepper

rice, to serve

Heat the oil in a large flameproof casserole over a moderate heat, add the pork in batches and brown well all over. Reduce the heat, add the onion, garlic and paprika and cook for 5–6 minutes until the onion has softened.

Add the wine, vinegar, bay leaf and red peppers. Bring to the boil, then season with salt and pepper. Reduce the heat, cover the casserole with a tight-fitting lid and cook gently for 30–35 minutes until the meat is tender. Check occasionally, adding more wine if the stew looks dry.

Add the clams, cover the casserole and cook for 3–5 minutes until they have opened; discard any that have not opened. To serve, sprinkle the stew with the chopped coriander, season to taste with salt and pepper and serve with rice.

peppered pork

Chorizo has a strong, distinctive flavour and the oil released from the sausage
will infuse the whole dish.

SERVES 2

1 tablespoon olive oil

300 g/10 oz pork shoulder steaks, diced

1 onion, sliced

½ red pepper, cored, deseeded and sliced

½ yellow pepper, cored, deseeded and
  sliced

½ green pepper, cored, deseeded and
  sliced

2 garlic cloves, chopped (optional)

1 tablespoon plain flour

200 g/7 oz can tomatoes

300 ml/½ pint Chicken Stock (see page 10)

75 g/3 oz chorizo sausage, sliced

300 g/10 oz new potatoes, scrubbed,
  and halved if large

salt and pepper

chopped parsley, to garnish

Heat the oil in a flameproof casserole. Add the pork and onion and
fry for 5 minutes, stirring until browned.

Add the peppers to the casserole with the garlic, if using, and fry for
1 minute. Stir in the flour, then add the tomatoes, stock, chorizo and
potatoes. Season to taste with salt and pepper. Bring to the boil, then
cover the casserole and transfer to a preheated oven, 180°C (350°F),
Gas Mark 4, and cook for 1½ hours. To serve, ladle the stew into bowls
and sprinkle with parsley.

FOOD **FACT**
High in vitamin C, peppers are great for boosting the immune system.
A green pepper provides twice as much vitamin C as a citrus fruit, and
a red pepper provides three times as much.

one pot pork roast

If you have time, try poaching some small dessert apples in a little water to serve with the pork.

SERVES 4

4 pork chops
6 sage leaves, chopped
2 teaspoons wholegrain mustard
grated rind and juice of ½ lemon
2 garlic cloves, crushed
4 tablespoons olive oil
3 baking potatoes
400 g/13 oz carrots
400 g/13 oz parsnips
salt and pepper
green vegetable, to serve

Trim the fat from the pork. Mix together the sage leaves, mustard, lemon rind and juice, garlic, a dash of the oil, and salt and pepper. Brush over the pork chops and set aside.

Cut the potatoes into small roasting-sized pieces and cut the carrots and parsnips into wedges. Parboil the vegetables in lightly salted boiling water for 5 minutes, then drain thoroughly.

Tip the vegetables into a large roasting tin, add the remaining oil and toss well. Roast in a preheated oven, 200°C (400°F), Gas Mark 6, for 15 minutes.

Add the pork chops to the roasting tin and return it to the oven for 35–40 minutes until the chops are cooked through and the vegetables are lightly browned. If you like, serve with a green vegetable such as broccoli, green beans or cabbage.

sausages with lentils

Unlike most other pulses, Puy lentils do not need to be soaked before cooking so this is a quick dish to prepare.

SERVES 4

75 g/3 oz pancetta or streaky bacon, cut into small strips

8 Italian sausages or other good-quality pork sausages

1 large red onion, sliced

2 garlic cloves, sliced

1 tablespoon chopped sage

250 ml/8 fl oz dry white wine

250 g/8 oz Puy lentils

175 g/6 oz pitted dried prunes

600 ml/1 pint water

salt and pepper

Heat a large flameproof casserole, without oil, over a low heat, add the pancetta or bacon and cook for 1–2 minutes until it renders some fat. Add the sausages and brown lightly all over. Add the onion, garlic and sage and cook gently until the onion has softened.

Increase the heat, add the wine and bring to the boil. Stir in the lentils, prunes and water, then bring back to the boil. Cover the casserole with a tight-fitting lid and transfer to a preheated oven, 180°C (350°F), Gas Mark 4, for 30 minutes, until the lentils are tender.

FOOD **FACT**
Pancetta is an Italian ham that will add a lovely rich, smoky flavour to this dish. The oil in the pancetta will also help to cook the other ingredients and means that you don't need to add any extra.

sausage and bean casserole

This hearty meal is ideal when time is in short supply. It uses lots of store-cupboard ingredients as well.

SERVES 4

1 tablespoon oil

1 onion, chopped

1 garlic clove, crushed

1 red pepper, cored, deseeded and chopped

4 lean pork sausages, quartered

2 x 410 g/13½ oz cans mixed beans, drained and rinsed

410 g/13½ oz can chopped tomatoes

150 ml/¼ pint Vegetable Stock (see page 11)

2 tablespoons tomato purée

2 tablespoons chopped parsley

salt and pepper

Heat the oil in a saucepan, add the onion, garlic and red pepper and fry for 2–3 minutes until they are beginning to soften.

Add the sausages and continue to cook for 5 minutes until browned all over.

Lightly crush half of the beans with the back of a fork and add to the pan with the remaining beans, the tomatoes, stock and tomato purée. Season to taste with salt and pepper. Bring to the boil and simmer for 10 minutes. Remove the pan from the heat, stir in the parsley and serve.

FOOD **FACT**

Beans are full of fibre and their bulk makes them a hearty addition to casseroles and hotpots. Once lightly crushed, they will also soak up all the lovely flavours in this dish.

beef and prune casserole

The wine and prunes add a wonderfully rich flavour to this meaty casserole, served with mashed potatoes to mop up the sauce.

SERVES 4

4 tablespoons olive oil

1–1.25 kg/2–2½ lb stewing beef, cut into 2.5 cm/1 inch cubes

1 onion, sliced

125 g/4 oz unsmoked back bacon, chopped

3 garlic cloves, crushed

1½ tablespoons plain flour

250 ml/8 fl oz Beef Stock (see page 12)

1 teaspoon ground cinnamon

1 thyme sprig

1 bay leaf

rind and juice of 1 large orange

250 g/8 oz tomatoes, skinned and chopped

2 tablespoons chopped parsley

125 ml/4 fl oz dry white wine

250 g/8 oz pitted dried prunes

salt and pepper

mashed potatoes, to serve

Heat the oil in a large flameproof casserole, add the meat in batches and brown well all over. Remove with a slotted spoon and set aside.

Add the onion, bacon and garlic to the casserole and cook until the onion is golden brown. Add the flour, stirring to blend it with the oil, and cook for 1–2 minutes; do not let it burn.

Add all the remaining ingredients and the reserved meat with any juices and stir gently to mix. Bring to the boil, reduce the heat and simmer gently, covered with a tight-fitting lid, for 1½–2 hours until the meat is tender. Check occasionally and add more stock or wine if the stew seems dry. Alternatively, cook in a preheated oven, 160°C (325°F), Gas Mark 3.

When the meat is cooked, if the sauce is too thin, remove the meat with a slotted spoon and keep it warm while you boil the sauce, uncovered, until it thickens. Serve hot, with mashed potatoes.

one-pot beef

This is a great way to cook beef as the liquid will ensure that the meat remains moist and tender.

SERVES 4–5

1 onion, sliced

750 g/1½ lb topside of beef, trimmed of fat

4 small baking potatoes, quartered

250 g/8 oz carrots, cut into chunks

250 g/8 oz parsnips, cut into chunks

50 g/2 oz pearl barley

2 bay leaves

900 ml/1½ pints Beef Stock or
    Chicken Stock (see pages 12 and 10)

1 tablespoon tomato purée

1 teaspoon wholegrain mustard

100 g/3½ oz green beans

1 small green cabbage heart, cut into
    8 wedges

salt and pepper

chopped parsley or thyme, to garnish

Put the onion into a large flameproof casserole and stand the beef joint on top. Add the potatoes, carrots and parsnips to the casserole with the pearl barley and bay leaves.

Pour the stock into the casserole and add the tomato purée, mustard and salt and pepper. Bring to the boil on the hob, then cover the casserole and transfer it to a preheated oven, 160°C (325°F), Gas Mark 3, and cook for 40 minutes for rare beef, 50 minutes for medium and 60 minutes for well done.

Lift the beef out of the casserole, put it on a plate and wrap it in foil to keep it warm. Add the green vegetables to the casserole. Cover the casserole and simmer on the hob for 5–8 minutes until the vegetables are just tender and still bright green.

Thinly slice the beef and arrange it on warm plates, lift the vegetables out of the casserole with a slotted spoon and arrange them around the beef. Spoon the gravy over the meat and garnish the vegetables with chopped herbs.

clam, potato and bean stew

Shellfish stews are quite unusual but really delicious. Make sure the clams or mussels are scrubbed well and discard any that are already open.

SERVES 6

2 tablespoons olive oil

125 g/4 oz piece of unsmoked pancetta, diced

1 onion, chopped

375 g/12 oz potatoes, cubed

1 leek, sliced

2 garlic cloves, crushed

1 tablespoon chopped rosemary

2 bay leaves

410 g/13½ oz can cannellini beans, drained

900 ml/1½ pints Vegetable Stock (see page 11)

1 kg/2 lb small clams or mussels, scrubbed

salt and pepper

crusty bread, to serve

Heat the oil in a large saucepan and fry the pancetta for 5 minutes, until golden. Remove from the pan with a slotted spoon and set aside. Add the onion, potatoes, leek, garlic, rosemary and bay leaves to the pan and fry gently for 10 minutes, until softened. Add the beans and stock, bring to the boil and simmer gently for 20 minutes, until the vegetables are tender.

Transfer half of the stew to a food processor and whizz until really smooth, then pour it back into the pan and season with salt and pepper to taste. Stir in the clams or mussels and add the pancetta to the stew. Simmer gently for about 5 minutes until the shellfish are open, discarding any that remain closed.

Spoon the stew into warm bowls and serve with some crusty bread.

cambodian fish hotpot

Coconut water comes from a green coconut or it can be bought in small cans in oriental stores as a ready-prepared drink.

SERVES 4

1 teaspoon sesame oil

1 tablespoon vegetable oil

3 shallots, chopped

3 garlic cloves, crushed

1 onion, halved and sliced

600 ml/1 pint coconut water

3 tablespoons rice wine vinegar

1 lemon grass stalk, chopped

4 kaffir lime leaves

6 red bird chillies

300 ml/½ pint Fish Stock (see page 13) or water

1 tablespoon caster sugar

2 tomatoes, quartered

4 tablespoons fish sauce

1 teaspoon tomato purée

375 g/12 oz tiger prawns, heads removed and peeled

125 g/4 oz squid, cleaned and cut into rings

175 g/6 oz clams, scrubbed

400 g/13 oz can straw mushrooms, drained

20 holy basil leaves

TO SERVE

rice noodles

Nuoc Mam or other oriental dipping sauce

handful of coriander leaves

Heat the sesame and vegetable oils together in a large flameproof casserole, add the shallots and garlic and fry gently for 2 minutes, or until softened but not browned.

Add the onion, coconut water, rice wine vinegar, lemon grass, lime leaves, chillies, stock and sugar to the casserole, bring to the boil and boil for 2 minutes. Reduce the heat and add the tomatoes, fish sauce and tomato purée and cook for 5 minutes.

Just before serving add the prawns, squid rings, clams and mushrooms to the casserole and simmer gently for 5–6 minutes, or until the seafood is cooked. Stir in the basil leaves.

Serve the hotpot immediately with rice noodles. Each diner ladles stock on to their noodles and seafood, then adds dipping sauce to taste, and some coriander leaves.

quick pesto pea
and broccoli soup

As the name suggests, this soup really is quick to prepare – perfect for a warming lunch or supper snack in the winter.

SERVES 4

2 tablespoons olive oil

1 onion, finely chopped

1 baking potato, about 275 g/9 oz, diced

1 garlic clove, chopped

200 g/7 oz can tomatoes

900 ml/1½ pints Vegetable Stock or
   Chicken Stock (see pages 11 and 10)

175 g/6 oz broccoli, cut into tiny florets
   and stalks sliced

125 g/4 oz frozen peas

2 teaspoons pesto

salt and pepper

TO GARNISH

extra pesto

freshly grated Parmesan cheese

a few basil leaves

Heat the oil in a large heavy-based saucepan, add the onion and fry for 5 minutes, until lightly browned. Add the potato and garlic and fry for 5 further minutes, stirring, until softened.

Add the tomatoes, stock and salt and pepper, then bring to the boil. Cover the pan and simmer for 10 minutes, until reduced and thickened. Add the broccoli, peas and pesto and simmer for 3–4 minutes, until the broccoli is just tender.

Ladle the soup into warm bowls, and garnish with a little extra pesto and sprinkle with some Parmesan and basil leaves.

FOOD **FACT**
Made with olive oil, basil and pine kernels, pesto is a versatile ingredient that adds a depth of flavour to soups, sauces and dressings. Stir a couple of teaspoons into pasta for a quick sauce or spread a little on bread when making a sandwich.

gingered butternut squash
and sweet potato soup

Velvety smooth, with a wonderful vibrant colour, this soup makes an ideal quick lunch and is smart enough to serve to friends, if dressed up with a swirl of cream.

SERVES 6

2 tablespoons olive oil

1 large onion, finely chopped

1 butternut squash, about 875 g/1¾ lb, deseeded and cut into chunks

1 sweet potato, about 300 g/10 oz, cut into chunks

3.5 cm/1½ inch piece of fresh root ginger, peeled and finely chopped

2 garlic cloves, chopped (optional)

900 ml/1½ pints Vegetable Stock or Chicken Stock (see pages 11 and 10)

450 ml/¾ pint semi-skimmed milk

salt and pepper

warm croûtons, to serve

Heat the oil in a large heavy-based saucepan, add the onion and fry for 5 minutes, until lightly browned. Add the squash, sweet potato, ginger and garlic, if using, and fry for 3 minutes, stirring.

Pour in the stock, season with salt and pepper and bring to the boil. Cover the pan and simmer for 30 minutes, until reduced and thickened. Purée the soup in a liquidizer or food processor until smooth. Return the soup to the pan and stir in the milk, then reheat the soup. To serve, ladle the soup into warm bowls and sprinkle with warm croûtons.

FOOD **FACT**
A little bit of ginger goes a long way but the flavour is amazing. A good way to prepare ginger is to cut away the tough skin and then grate it, using the larger slots of a cheese grater. The flesh is quite fibrous so it can sometimes be difficult to cut with a knife.

spicy lentil and tomato soup

A vegetarian soup that packs a punch. This is a great one to have in the freezer, so make double and freeze what you don't use.

SERVES 4

1 tablespoon vegetable oil

1 large onion, finely chopped

2 garlic cloves, finely chopped

1 small green chilli, deseeded and finely chopped (optional)

250 g/8 oz red lentils, washed and drained

1 bay leaf

3 celery sticks, thinly sliced

3 carrots, thinly sliced

1 leek, thinly sliced

1.5 litres/2½ pints Vegetable Stock (see page 11)

410 g/13½ oz can chopped tomatoes

2 tablespoons tomato purée

½ teaspoon ground turmeric

½ teaspoon ground ginger

1 tablespoon chopped coriander leaves

pepper

natural yogurt, to garnish

crusty wholemeal bread, to serve (optional)

Heat the oil in a large saucepan, add the onion, garlic and chilli, if using, and fry gently for 4–5 minutes until softened.

Add the lentils, bay leaf, celery, carrots, leek and stock. Cover the pan and bring to the boil, then reduce the heat and simmer for 30–40 minutes until the lentils are soft. Remove the bay leaf.

Stir in the tomatoes, tomato purée, turmeric, ginger, coriander leaves and pepper to taste. Allow the soup to cool a little, then transfer it to a liquidizer or food processor. Whizz until smooth, adding more stock or water if necessary.

Reheat the soup gently, then pour it into warm bowls and garnish with a swirl of yogurt. Serve with crusty wholemeal bread, if liked.

sweet potato and coconut soup

You can use 600 ml/1 pint water and a 400 ml/14 fl oz can of coconut milk, but, naturally, if you use fresh coconut milk it will be all the better.

SERVES 4–6

1 small coconut

1 litre/1¾ pints boiling water

4 tablespoons olive oil

2 onions, finely chopped

500 g/1 lb sweet potatoes, peeled and roughly chopped

2 garlic cloves, crushed

7 cm/3 inch piece of fresh root ginger, peeled and finely chopped

¼ teaspoon dried chilli flakes

sea salt and pepper

Using a corkscrew, drill holes in the three eyes at the top of the coconut. Pour the liquid out of the eyes and reserve. Crack open the coconut, prise out the flesh and grate it roughly.

Put the grated coconut into a bowl with the boiling water and leave to stand for 1 hour to cool. Squeeze and rub the grated coconut into the water, as if washing, to extract as much of the juice and oil from the coconut flesh as you can. Strain the liquid into a jug and reserve 2 tablespoons of the coconut pulp.

Heat the oil and gently fry the onions for about 10 minutes, or until golden brown. Add the chopped sweet potato flesh and fry for 4–5 minutes, or until it has begun to brown.

Add the crushed garlic, chopped root ginger, dried chilli and the reserved coconut water and white coconut milk. Add the 2 tablespoons coconut pulp and salt and pepper and bring to a fast simmer, but do not boil. Cover the pan and simmer for 30–35 minutes.

When the sweet potato is tender, purée it in a food processor, then return it to the pan. Check the seasoning once more, then heat through thoroughly and serve.

bright red pepper soup

A vibrant and warming soup, which makes an ideal start for any meal and tastes just as good warm or cold.

SERVES 4

2 tablespoons groundnut or olive oil

2 onions, finely chopped

1 garlic clove, crushed (optional)

3 red peppers, cored, deseeded and
    roughly chopped

2 courgettes, roughly chopped

900 ml/1½ pints Vegetable Stock
    (see page 11) or water

sea salt and pepper

TO SERVE

natural yogurt or double cream

chopped chives

Heat the oil in a large saucepan, add the onions and fry gently for 5 minutes, or until softened and golden brown. Add the garlic, if using, and cook gently for 1 minute.

Add all the red peppers and half the courgettes to the pan. Fry for 5–8 minutes, or until softened and brown.

Add the stock with salt and pepper to taste and bring to the boil. Reduce the heat, cover the pan and simmer gently for 20 minutes.

When the vegetables are tender, tip the mixture into a liquidizer or food processor and whizz until smooth, then return to the pan. Season to taste with salt and pepper, then reheat the soup and serve in warm bowls topped with the remaining chopped courgette, a swirl of yogurt or double cream and chopped chives.

tomato and bread soup

Bread soups are a popular Italian tradition, resulting in a more substantial dish with that lovely, rough texture.

SERVES 4

1 kg/2 lb vine-ripened tomatoes, skinned, deseeded and chopped

300 ml/½ pint Vegetable Stock (see page 11)

6 tablespoons olive oil

2 garlic cloves, crushed

1 teaspoon sugar

2 tablespoons chopped basil

100 g/3½ oz day-old bread, without crusts

1 tablespoon balsamic vinegar

salt and pepper

pesto, to serve (optional)

Put the tomatoes into a large saucepan with the stock, 2 tablespoons of the oil, the garlic, sugar and basil and bring to the boil gradually. Lower the heat, cover and simmer gently for 30 minutes.

Crumble the bread into the soup and stir over a low heat until it has thickened. Stir in the balsamic vinegar and the remaining oil and season to taste with salt and pepper. Stir a spoonful of pesto into each warm bowl before serving, if liked.

minestrone verde with red pesto

Make extra pesto – it will keep in the refrigerator for a few days and will make a great dip or pasta sauce.

SERVES 4–6

50 g/2 oz dried haricot or cannellini beans, soaked overnight

3 tablespoons olive oil

2 garlic cloves, crushed

1 celery stick, finely chopped

2 leeks, sliced into rings

3 tomatoes, skinned and chopped

3 tablespoons chopped flat leaf parsley

½ tablespoon snipped chives

125 g/4 oz green beans, cut into 2.5 cm/ 1 inch pieces

150 g/5 oz shelled broad beans, defrosted if frozen, popped out of their skins

125 g/4 oz shelled peas, fresh or frozen

1 litre/1¾ pints Vegetable Stock or Chicken Stock (see pages 11 and 10) or boiling water

75 g/3 oz long-grain rice

175 g/6 oz fresh spinach

salt and pepper

snipped chives, to garnish

50 g/2 oz Parmesan cheese, freshly grated, to serve

RED PESTO

2 garlic cloves, chopped

25 g/1 oz basil leaves

3 tablespoons pine nuts

8 sun-dried tomatoes in oil, drained

125 ml/4 fl oz olive oil

25 g/1 oz Parmesan cheese, freshly grated

salt and pepper

Drain and rinse the haricot or cannellini beans, put them into a saucepan and cover with cold water. Bring to the boil, then reduce the heat and simmer for 45–60 minutes, or until tender. Remove the beans from the heat and set aside in their cooking liquid.

To make the pesto, whizz the garlic, basil, pine nuts and sun-dried tomatoes in a liquidizer or food processor until finely chopped. With the motor running, gradually add the olive oil in a thin stream until amalgamated. Scrape into a bowl, stir in the Parmesan and season to taste with salt and pepper.

Put the oil into a large saucepan, add the garlic, celery and leeks and cook gently for 5–10 minutes until softened. Add the chopped tomatoes with half of the parsley and chives, season with salt and pepper and cook until the tomatoes become pulpy – about 12–15 minutes.

Add the green beans and the broad beans and the peas if using fresh ones. Cook for 1–2 minutes, then add the stock or water. Bring to the boil and boil rapidly for 10 minutes. Add the rice, the cooked haricot or cannellini beans and their cooking liquid and the spinach (and the broad beans and peas, if using frozen ones) and cook for 10 minutes. Adjust the seasoning to taste and stir in the remaining parsley and chives.

To serve, pour into warm bowls and garnish each one with a spoonful of pesto, a few chives, and sprinkled with some Parmesan.

borscht with apple

Some people like to add soured cream to this version of the traditional Russian soup just before serving. If you are serving the soup chilled, add a spoonful of thick natural yogurt.

SERVES 4–6

500 g/1 lb raw beetroot
1 small fennel bulb
600 ml/1 pint water
600 ml/1 pint apple juice
1 teaspoon thyme leaves
4 tablespoons lemon juice
1 tablespoon chopped chives
sea salt and pepper
soda bread, to serve

Peel the beetroot and cut the flesh into thin matchsticks. Be careful of the juice as it stains clothes and will stain your hands as you peel the skin and cut into the flesh.

Trim the fennel and cut the bulb into strips. Put the beetroot and fennel into a large saucepan with the water and bring slowly to the boil. Cover the pan and simmer gently for 20–30 minutes or until the vegetables are tender.

Add the apple juice, thyme leaves and salt and pepper and simmer for 10 minutes. Remove the pan from the heat and add the lemon juice and chopped chives. Season to taste with salt and pepper and serve the soup hot, warm or cold with soda bread.

FOOD **FACT**
Fennel has a strong aniseed flavour and is actually a member of the parsley family. The seeds of the plant are also used as a flavouring and they are traditionally eaten after meals in India to aid digestion.

harira

This is the soup eaten during the holy month of Ramadan in Muslim countries throughout North Africa and the Middle East.

SERVES 8

1.5 kg/3 lb free-range chicken
2–4 tablespoons olive oil
1 onion, chopped
4 garlic cloves, crushed
1 teaspoon grated fresh root ginger
2 teaspoons hot paprika
¼ teaspoon saffron threads
2 x 410 g/13½ oz cans chopped tomatoes
900 ml/1½ pints water
125 g/4 oz cooked chickpeas (from a can)
50 g/2 oz red lentils
50 g/2 oz basmati rice
juice of 1 lemon
2 tablespoons each chopped parsley and
    coriander
1–2 tablespoons harissa (optional)
salt and pepper
pitta bread, to serve

Joint the chicken into 8 pieces. Heat the oil in a saucepan and brown the chicken pieces on all sides. Remove with a slotted spoon.

Add more oil to the pan if necessary, then add the onion, garlic and ginger and fry gently for 10 minutes, until they are lightly golden. Return the chicken to the pan and add all the remaining ingredients except the parsley, coriander and harissa, if using. Cover the pan and simmer gently for 45 minutes.

Pick out the chicken pieces, leave them to cool slightly, then gently pull the flesh away from the bones and return it to the soup. Leave the soup to cool completely, then cover and chill overnight.

Reheat the soup, stir in the parsley and coriander and harissa, if using, and serve with warm pitta bread.

FOOD **FACT**
Harissa is a hot spicy paste, made with chillies, that's used in many Moroccan dishes. If you're not familiar with it, add to the soup with caution. You can always add a little more later on if you like.

moroccan fish soup

Any selection of fish and shellfish can be used for this fish soup, with the exception of oily fish such as mackerel and sardines.

SERVES 6–8

3 tablespoons olive oil

2 onions, chopped

2 celery sticks, sliced

4 garlic cloves, crushed

1 fresh red chilli, deseeded and chopped

½ teaspoon ground cumin

1 cinnamon stick

½ teaspoon ground coriander

2 large potatoes, chopped

1.5 litres/2½ pints Fish Stock
   (see page 13), or water

3 tablespoons lemon juice

2 kg/4 lb mixed fish and shellfish,
   prepared

4 well-flavoured tomatoes, skinned,
   deseeded and chopped

1 large bunch mixed dill, parsley and
   coriander, chopped

salt and pepper

Heat the oil in a large saucepan. Add the onions and celery and fry gently until softened, adding the garlic and chilli towards the end. Add the cumin, cinnamon and coriander and stir for 1 minute, then add the potatoes and cook, stirring, for a further 2 minutes.

Add the stock or water and the lemon juice. Heat to simmering point, then simmer gently, uncovered, for about 20 minutes until the potatoes are tender.

Add the fish and shellfish, the tomatoes, herbs and salt and pepper and cook gently until the fish and shellfish are done.

creamy haddock and
spinach chowder

American-style chowders are among the easiest soups to prepare, since the vegetables and fish are simply poached in milk, resulting in a creamy, satisfying, calcium-packed soup.

SERVES 3

25 g/1 oz butter

1 tablespoon sunflower oil

1 onion, chopped

1 medium baking potato, diced

600 ml/1 pint semi-skimmed milk

1 fish stock cube

2 bay leaves

freshly grated nutmeg

1 undyed smoked haddock fillet, about 250 g/8 oz, halved

125 g/4 oz young spinach leaves, stems removed and torn into pieces

salt and pepper

4 grilled rindless streaky bacon rashers, to garnish (optional)

crusty bread, to serve

Heat the butter and oil in a large heavy-based saucepan, add the onion and fry gently for 5 minutes, until softened but not browned. Add the potato and fry for a further 5 minutes, stirring, until lightly browned.

Stir in the milk, stock cube, bay leaves, nutmeg and salt and pepper to taste. Add the haddock, then bring to the boil, cover the pan and simmer for 10 minutes, until the haddock is cooked and flakes easily.

Lift the haddock out of the pan on to a plate, peel off the skin and flake the flesh into pieces, carefully removing any bones, then set aside.

Add the spinach to the pan and cook for 2–3 minutes, until tender. Return the haddock to the pan and reheat.

Cut the grilled bacon into strips. Ladle the soup into warm bowls and garnish with the bacon, if using. Serve with crusty bread.

international inspiration

One-pot cooking is popular in countries all over the world for its ease and lack of complicated cooking techniques and equipment. The meal virtually prepares itself, freeing up valuable time to do other things. Here's a tempting collection of dishes that are ideal for laid-back entertaining. What guest won't be impressed with *Catalan Beef Stew with Chocolate* or *Thai Monkfish and Prawn Curry*?

moroccan red chicken

It's the paprika that adds the red colour to this dish. The fresh zing of the coriander and lemon juice really complements the spices.

SERVES 4

75 g/3 oz unsalted butter

4 chicken joints

1 onion, chopped

1 teaspoon black peppercorns, crushed

2 teaspoons paprika

1 teaspoon cumin seeds

5 cm/2 inch cinnamon stick

1 tablespoon chopped coriander leaves

juice of 1 lemon

salt

Heat 25 g/1 oz of the butter in a large flameproof casserole. Add the chicken and brown evenly. Remove to kitchen paper to drain.

Put the onion into the casserole and fry gently until softened and translucent. Add the peppercorns, paprika, cumin and cinnamon and return the chicken pieces to the casserole. Pour in enough water to just cover the chicken, then cover the casserole with a tight-fitting lid and simmer gently for about 1 hour, turning the chicken pieces over a couple of times.

Transfer the chicken to a warm platter. Boil the cooking juices hard until reduced by half, then strain the juices and stir in the coriander and lemon juice. Season with salt to taste. Pour the juices over the chicken and serve.

FOOD **FACT**

Available as seeds or ground, cumin is used extensively in North African and Indian cooking, as a flavouring. The seeds are usually dry-fried, then crushed, using a pestle and mortar, before being added to the dish. This releases the flavours of the spice.

chicken cacciatore

Try to use the best wine you can for this dish – you'll notice the difference this will make in the flavour.

SERVES 4

3–4 tablespoons olive oil

1.5 kg/3 lb chicken, cut into pieces or
    8 chicken thighs

50 g/2 oz fat bacon, diced

1 onion, finely chopped

1 garlic clove, crushed

1 teaspoon flour

125 ml/4 fl oz dry white wine

250 ml/8 fl oz Chicken Stock
    (see page 10)

4 ripe tomatoes, skinned, deseeded,
    and sliced

1 teaspoon tomato purée

125 g/4 oz mushrooms, quartered

salt and pepper

chopped flat leaf parsley and flat leaf
    parsley sprigs, to serve

Heat 2 tablespoons of the oil in a large flameproof casserole and brown the chicken pieces on all sides. Remove from the casserole and add the bacon. Cook until golden brown, then remove from the casserole. Add more oil if necessary and cook the onion and garlic gently until golden brown. Stir in the flour and cook for a few moments, then add the white wine, stock, tomatoes and tomato purée. Bring to the boil and season lightly with salt and pepper.

Return the chicken and bacon to the casserole. Cover tightly and cook in a preheated oven, 190°C (375°F) Gas Mark 5, for 25–30 minutes. Add the mushrooms and continue cooking for 10–15 minutes, until the chicken and mushrooms are tender.

Transfer the chicken pieces to a warm serving dish, cover and keep warm. If necessary, boil the sauce to reduce it to a coating consistency. Pour the sauce over the chicken and sprinkle with the parsley. Garnish the dish with the parsley sprigs just before serving.

chicken, lemon and olive stew

This is a Moroccan dish using preserved lemons, a bitter pickle which they add to many of their meat dishes. Preserved lemons can be bought from North African and Middle Eastern stores and some supermarkets.

SERVES 4

2.25 kg/4½ lb free-range chicken

about 4 tablespoons olive oil

12 baby onions, peeled but left whole

2 garlic cloves, crushed

1 teaspoon each ground cumin, ginger
   and turmeric

½ teaspoon ground cinnamon

450 ml/¾ pint Chicken Stock
   (see page 10)

125 g/4 oz Kalamata olives

1 preserved lemon, chopped

2 tablespoons chopped coriander leaves

salt and pepper

cooked couscous, rice or pasta, to serve

Joint the chicken into eight pieces. Heat the oil in a large flameproof casserole and brown the chicken on all sides. Remove the pieces with a slotted spoon and set aside.

Add the onions, garlic, cumin, ginger, turmeric and cinnamon and fry over a low heat for 10 minutes, until just golden. Return the chicken to the casserole, stir in the stock and bring to the boil. Cover and simmer gently for 30 minutes.

Add the olives, chopped lemon and coriander and cook for 15–20 minutes, until the chicken is really tender. Taste and adjust the seasoning, if necessary, and serve with couscous, rice or pasta.

chicken biryani

If you have more time, allow the chicken to marinate for longer. Just cover the bowl with clingfilm, then place in the refrigerator.

SERVES 4

250 g/8 oz chicken thighs, skinned and boned

1 teaspoon turmeric

1 teaspoon ground cumin

1 teaspoon ground coriander

1 teaspoon chilli powder

6 tablespoons Greek yogurt

1 tablespoon vegetable oil

1 onion, thinly sliced

2 garlic cloves, finely chopped

1 teaspoon grated fresh root ginger

5 cm/2 inch piece of cinnamon stick

3 cloves

3 cardamom pods

250 g/8 oz basmati rice

600 ml/1 pint Chicken Stock (see page 10)

400 g/13 oz potatoes, cut into 2.5 cm/ 1 inch chunks

salt and pepper

TO SERVE

tomato and cucumber salad

poppadums

Indian pickles or chutneys

Cut the chicken into bite-sized pieces and put them in a bowl. Add the turmeric, cumin, coriander, chilli and yogurt and mix well.

Heat the oil in a heavy-based saucepan. Add the onion, garlic, ginger, cinnamon, cloves and cardamoms and fry for 3–4 minutes.

Add the chicken mixture and cook for 2–3 minutes, stirring often. Then stir in the rice and pour in the stock. Season generously with salt and pepper and bring to the boil. Add the potatoes, cover the pan tightly and reduce the heat. Simmer gently for 10–12 minutes.

Remove the pan from the heat and leave it to stand, without removing the lid, for 5 minutes. Fluff up the rice with a fork and serve the biryani with a tomato and cucumber salad, poppadums and Indian pickles or chutneys.

thai chicken curry

The lemon grass and kaffir lime leaves give this dish a really light, fresh flavour. Serve with basmati rice, which is a delicate grain.

SERVES 4

1 tablespoon sunflower oil

1 lemon grass stalk, cut into 4 pieces

2 kaffir lime leaves, halved

1–2 red chillies, finely chopped

2.5 cm/1 inch piece of fresh root ginger, peeled and grated

1 onion, finely chopped

1 garlic clove, crushed

1 red pepper, cored, deseeded and chopped

1 green pepper, cored, deseeded and chopped

3 boneless, skinless chicken breasts, chopped

410 g/13½ oz can coconut milk

150 ml/¼ pint Chicken Stock (see page 10)

2 tablespoons chopped coriander leaves

salt and pepper

basmati rice, to serve

Heat the oil in a saucepan, add the lemon grass, lime leaves, chilli, ginger, onion and garlic and fry for 2 minutes. Add the red and green peppers and chopped chicken and fry for 5 minutes.

Pour in the coconut milk and the stock and simmer for 10 minutes, or until the chicken is cooked through.

Stir in the coriander leaves and season to taste with salt and pepper. Serve with rice.

FOOD **FACT**
Lemon grass is often used as a flavouring in Thai and other Asian dishes. You can either add the whole stalk, removing it before serving or, as is more often the case, finely chop it and add to the dish while cooking. You need to trim the ends and remove the tough outer layer first.

chicken and spinach masala

Chicken and spinach are a classic combination and this fragrant Indian recipe uses a variety of spices to enrich the sauce.

SERVES 4

2 tablespoons vegetable oil

1 onion, thinly sliced

2 garlic cloves, crushed

1 green chilli, deseeded and thinly sliced

1 teaspoon finely grated fresh root ginger

1 teaspoon ground coriander

1 teaspoon ground cumin

200 g/7 oz can tomatoes

750 g/1¾ lb chicken thighs, skinned, boned and cut into bite-sized pieces

200 ml/7 fl oz crème fraîche

300 g/10 oz spinach, roughly chopped

2 tablespoons chopped coriander leaves

salt and pepper

TO SERVE

warmed naan bread or boiled basmati rice

chutneys or fresh mixed salad

Heat the oil in a large heavy-based saucepan. Add the onion, garlic, chilli and ginger. Stir-fry for 2–3 minutes and then add the ground coriander and cumin. Stir and cook for 1 minute.

Pour in the tomatoes with their juice and cook gently for 3 minutes. Increase the heat and add the chicken. Cook, stirring, until the outside of the chicken pieces are sealed. Stir in the crème fraîche and spinach.

Cover the pan and cook the chicken mixture gently for 6–8 minutes, stirring occasionally. Stir in the coriander with salt and pepper to taste. Serve hot with naan bread or basmati rice, chutneys or a mixed salad.

lamb with aubergines

Lamb is the meat used most widely in North African dishes and it suits long, slow cooking methods, as in this recipe.

SERVES 6

1 kg/2 lb shoulder of lamb, cut into 5 cm/2 inch cubes

750 g/1½ lb large onions, thinly sliced

5 garlic cloves, crushed

1 fresh red chilli, deseeded and finely chopped

5 cm/2 inch piece of fresh root ginger, peeled and grated

1 bay leaf, torn across

4 tablespoons olive oil

250 g/8 oz potatoes, cut into 2.5 cm/ 1 inch cubes

500 g/1 lb small aubergines, cut into 2.5 cm/1 inch cubes

2 red peppers, cored, deseeded and cut into strips

410 g/13½ oz can chopped tomatoes

salt and pepper

large handful of mixed parsley and coriander leaves, to garnish

Put the lamb into a large bowl, then stir in the onions, garlic, chilli, ginger, bay leaf and oil. Cover and leave in a cool place, not the refrigerator, for 4 hours. Alternatively, chill in the refrigerator overnight and return to room temperature 1 hour before cooking.

Stir the potatoes, aubergines, red peppers and the tomatoes with their juice into the lamb and season with salt and pepper. Transfer to a casserole that the ingredients just fit, cover and bake in a preheated oven, 200°C (400°F), Gas Mark 6, for 30 minutes.

Lower the oven temperature to 160°C (325°F), Gas Mark 3 and cook for 1½ hours, stirring once or twice, until the lamb is very tender. If necessary, add a little water or stock to the casserole.

To serve, scatter the parsley and coriander liberally over the casserole.

easy lamb tagine

Spicy lamb and plump dried apricots make a delicious combination in this simple version of a North African tagine.

SERVES 6

1 butternut squash

750 g/1½ lb lamb fillet

2 tablespoons plain flour

2 tablespoons olive oil

2 onions, chopped

3 celery sticks, sliced

3 garlic cloves, crushed

1 cinnamon stick, halved

450 ml/¾ pint Chicken Stock (see page 10) or lamb stock

410 g/13½ oz can chickpeas, rinsed and drained

75 g/3 oz ready-to-eat dried apricots, roughly chopped

2 teaspoons cumin seeds

1 red chilli, deseeded and finely chopped

4 tablespoons roughly chopped coriander leaves

salt and pepper

couscous, to serve

Halve the squash and discard the seeds and fibres. Cut away the skin and cut the flesh into small chunks.

Cut the lamb into small chunks, discarding any excess fat. Mix the flour with a little salt and pepper and use to coat the lamb.

Heat the oil in a large saucepan. Fry the lamb in batches until browned, then set aside. Add the onions, celery and garlic to the pan and fry for 3 minutes.

Return the meat to the pan. Add the cinnamon, stock, chickpeas, squash and apricots and bring just to the boil. Reduce the heat, cover the pan and simmer gently for 30 minutes until the lamb is tender. Stir in the cumin seeds, chilli and coriander and cook for 15 minutes.

Serve the tagine with couscous cooked according to packet instructions.

catalan beef stew with chocolate

The use of chocolate in a savoury dish usually implies that a recipe comes from the Catalan region of Spain. In this stew, it adds both a richness and a slight tartness.

SERVES 4

25 g/1 oz butter

4 tablespoons olive oil

1 kg/2 lb stewing beef, cubed

2 onions, chopped

4 garlic cloves, chopped

1 tablespoon plain flour

150 ml/¼ pint dry sherry

4 parsley sprigs

4 bay leaves

1 teaspoon each dried oregano and thyme

2 cinnamon sticks, crumbled

250 g/8 oz button mushrooms

15 g/½ oz bitter chocolate, chopped

250 g/8 oz waxy potatoes, cubed

salt and pepper

Heat the butter and 2 tablespoons of the oil in a large flameproof casserole, add the beef in batches and brown well on all sides. Stir in the onions and garlic and fry gently for 10 minutes, until they have softened, adding a little extra butter if necessary.

Sprinkle over the flour, stirring with a wooden spoon, and then gradually stir in the sherry. Bring to the boil and then add the parsley, bay leaves, oregano, thyme, cinnamon, a little salt and pepper and enough water to just cover the beef. Simmer gently, covered, for 2 hours.

Heat the remaining oil in a frying pan and fry the mushrooms for 3–4 minutes, until browned, then stir them into the stew with the chocolate and potatoes. Cook for 20–30 minutes, until the beef and potatoes are tender. Season with salt and pepper to taste.

FOOD **FACT**
Although chocolate may seem like an odd ingredient it actually works very well in stews, especially with red meat. You probably wouldn't recognize the flavour if you didn't know it was in there, but you'll notice a richness in the dish – make sure you use a bitter chocolate.

middle eastern beef casserole

Bulgar wheat is the traditional accompaniment to this dish; however, you could also serve it with couscous or rice.

SERVES 4–6

175 g/6 oz dried chickpeas, soaked overnight

3 tablespoons olive oil

1.5 kg/3 lb stewing beef, cut into 3.5 cm/1½ inch cubes

2 onions, sliced

2 garlic cloves, chopped

375 g/12 oz tomatoes, skinned and chopped

1 tablespoon tomato purée

1 teaspoon ground allspice

900 ml/1½ pints water

cayenne pepper

750 g/1½ lb courgettes, sliced

25 g/1 oz flat leaf parsley, chopped

salt and pepper

bulgar wheat, to serve

Drain the chickpeas and rinse well. Heat the oil in a large flameproof casserole over a moderate heat, add the meat in batches and brown well all over. Remove with a slotted spoon and set aside.

Reduce the heat, add the onions and garlic and cook for 5–6 minutes until softened. Return the meat to the pan and add the tomatoes, tomato purée, allspice and chickpeas. Cover with the water, stir well and bring to the boil. Season with salt, pepper and cayenne. Reduce the heat, cover the casserole with a tight-fitting lid and simmer gently for 1½ hours.

Add the courgettes and half of the parsley and cook for 15–20 minutes, stirring occasionally, until the meat is tender and the chickpeas are cooked. Stir in the remaining parsley and serve with bulgar wheat.

FOOD **FACT**
Chickpeas are available canned or dried and, in this instance, they will require soaking like other dried beans. They have a very thin skin covering them which can be removed if you prefer; however, it won't really make a big difference to your finished dish.

beef tagine

You could also use this tagine as the basis for a cottage pie, covering with mashed potato and browning under the grill.

SERVES 4

1 tablespoon olive oil

250 g/8 oz extra lean minced beef

1 onion, chopped

125 g/4 oz swede, diced

125 g/4 oz carrot, diced

½ teaspoon each of turmeric, ground cumin, cinnamon and mild chilli powder

1 garlic clove, chopped

200 g/7 oz can tomatoes

300 ml/½ pint Chicken Stock (see page 10)

200 g/7 oz canned chickpeas, drained and rinsed

2 tablespoons raisins or sultanas

75 g/3 oz frozen broad beans

50 g/2 oz frozen peas

salt and pepper

torn coriander leaves, to garnish (optional)

warm Middle Eastern bread or pitta bread, to serve

Heat the oil in a large flameproof casserole, add the beef and onion and fry, breaking up the mince with a wooden spoon, for 5 minutes, until browned.

Stir in the swede, carrot, spices and garlic and cook for 1 minute. Add the tomatoes, stock, chickpeas, raisins or sultanas and salt and pepper. Bring to the boil, stirring, then cover the casserole and transfer to a preheated oven, 180°C (350°F), Gas Mark 4, for 1½ hours.

Remove the casserole from the oven, add the frozen vegetables and stir well. Return the casserole to the oven for 10 minutes.

To serve, spoon the tagine into shallow dishes, sprinkle with coriander, if using, and serve with warm Middle Eastern bread or pitta bread.

orange osso buco

A popular Italian dish, this recipe uses fresh orange juice and dry white wine as the basis for the sauce.

SERVES 4

3 tablespoons plain flour

4 thick slices of shin of veal, of equal size (9 cm/3½ in diameter x 3.5 cm/1½ in thick)

2 tablespoons olive oil

25 g/1 oz butter

1 onion, very finely chopped

1 celery stick, finely chopped

1 carrot, finely chopped

200 g/7 oz can chopped tomatoes

1 thyme sprig

150 ml/¼ pint dry white wine

450–600 ml/¾–1 pint Chicken Stock (see page 10)

250 ml/8 fl oz fresh orange juice

salt and pepper

risotto, to serve

GREMOLATA

1 garlic clove, very finely chopped

4 tablespoons chopped flat leaf parsley

1 tablespoon finely grated orange rind

Season the flour with salt and pepper and roll the veal pieces in the flour, shaking off any excess. Tie a piece of string around each piece of veal to keep its shape.

Heat the oil and butter in a large flameproof casserole, add the veal pieces two at a time and brown well all over. Transfer to a plate. Add the onion, celery and carrot and cook gently for 10 minutes, stirring frequently. Add the tomatoes and thyme and place the veal on top. Add the wine and stock to just cover the meat, bring to the boil, then reduce the heat and simmer very gently, tightly covered, for 1½–2 hours until the veal is very tender, adding the orange juice after 1 hour. Baste occasionally and add more stock if necessary.

If the veal sauce is too thin, remove the meat with a slotted spoon and keep it warm, then boil the sauce, uncovered, until reduced and thickened slightly. Season to taste with salt and pepper.

Mix together all the ingredients for the gremolata, sprinkle it over the veal and serve hot, accompanied by a risotto.

thai monkfish and prawn curry

Tiger prawns are the best variety to use in a curry. They will literally cook in a couple of minutes in the sauce, so don't be tempted to add them any sooner.

SERVES 4

3 tablespoons Thai green curry paste

400 g/13½ oz can coconut milk

1 lemon grass stalk (optional)

2 kaffir lime leaves (optional)

1 tablespoon soft brown sugar

1 teaspoon salt

300 g/10 oz monkfish, cubed

75 g/3 oz green beans, trimmed

12 raw tiger prawns, peeled and deveined

3 tablespoons Thai fish sauce

2 tablespoons fresh lime juice

plain boiled rice, to serve

TO GARNISH

coriander sprigs

sliced green chillies

Put the curry paste and coconut milk in a saucepan with the lemon grass and lime leaves, if using, sugar and salt. Bring to the boil, then add the monkfish. Simmer gently for 2 minutes, then add the beans and cook for a further 2 minutes.

Remove the pan from the heat and stir in the prawns, fish sauce and lime juice. The prawns will cook in the residual heat, but you will need to push them under the liquid.

Transfer the curry to a warm serving dish and top with coriander sprigs and chilli slices. Serve with plain boiled rice.

FOOD **FACT**
A firm, meaty fish, monkfish is ideal for curries as its robust texture means it won't break up while cooking. It can also take lots of strong flavouring and works well here with the coconut milk and lemon grass.

north african fish stew

If you don't like gutting and scaling fish, either buy fillets or ask your fishmonger to prepare the fish for you.

SERVES 4–6

125 g/4 oz chickpeas, soaked overnight

4 tablespoons olive oil

2 onions, cut into small wedges but still attached to root

1–2 garlic cloves, sliced

1 celery stick, sliced

1 red or green pepper, cored, deseeded and cut into strips

1 teaspoon harissa

1 teaspoon ground cumin

375 g/12 oz ripe tomatoes, skinned and chopped

1 tablespoon tomato purée

2 carrots, sliced

large pinch of saffron threads

1.2 litres/2 pints Fish Stock or Chicken Stock (see pages 13 and 10)

500 g/1 lb couscous

1–1.25 kg/2–2½ lb firm white fish (bass, mullet, bream, snapper, cod), scaled, gutted and cut into large pieces

1½ tablespoons chopped parsley

1½ tablespoons chopped coriander leaves

salt and pepper

coriander sprigs, to garnish

Drain and rinse the chickpeas, put them into a saucepan and cover with water. Bring to the boil, then reduce the heat and simmer for 1 hour, or until tender. Drain.

Heat the oil in a large flameproof casserole, add the onion, garlic and celery and cook for 10–12 minutes, until softened and golden. Add the pepper, harissa and cumin and cook for 5 minutes. Add the tomatoes, tomato purée, carrots, saffron, stock and the drained chickpeas. Bring to the boil, reduce the heat and simmer gently for 15 minutes. Season to taste with salt and pepper.

Prepare the couscous according to the packet instructions and keep warm. Add the fish pieces to the stew and cook for 5 minutes, or until they are opaque. Stir in the parsley and coriander. Serve the stew spooned over the couscous and garnished with coriander sprigs.

mediterranean stew

An easy main meal soup-cum-stew, richly flavoured with tomato and served with a piquant spring onion pesto.

SERVES 4

5 tablespoons olive oil

500 g/1 lb lean lamb fillet, very thinly sliced

1 red onion, chopped

1 large aubergine, about 375 g/12 oz, cut into small chunks

2 garlic cloves, crushed

400 g/13½ oz can chopped tomatoes

2 tablespoons sun-dried tomato paste

1 teaspoon light muscovado sugar

150 ml/¼ pint Vegetable Stock (see page 11)

½ bunch of spring onions, trimmed and roughly chopped

50 g/2 oz Parmesan cheese, crumbled

2 teaspoons wine vinegar or fresh lemon juice

salt and pepper

snipped chives, to garnish

crusty bread, to serve

Heat 1 tablespoon of the oil in a large flameproof casserole. Add the lamb and fry gently for 5 minutes. Remove the lamb and set aside.

Heat a further 1 tablespoon of the oil in the casserole, add the onion and aubergine and fry for about 5 minutes until beginning to colour. Add the garlic, tomatoes, tomato paste, sugar and stock and bring to the boil. Reduce the heat, cover the pan and simmer gently for 5 minutes.

Return the lamb to the casserole and stir into the vegetables. Cook gently for 15 minutes. Check the seasoning.

Put the spring onions, Parmesan, vinegar or lemon juice and the remaining olive oil into a liquidizer or food processor and whizz to a coarse paste. Transfer this pesto to a small bowl.

Ladle the stew into warm soup bowls. Garnish with chives and serve with the pesto and crusty bread.

vegetable and barley stew
with dumplings

This is the ideal dish to come home to on a cold winter's day – so give everyone spoons to scoop up all the tasty gravy.

SERVES 4

1 tablespoon sunflower oil

1 onion, finely chopped

2 carrots, about 175 g/6 oz, chopped

1 small parsnip, about 150 g/5 oz, chopped

200 g/7 oz swede, chopped

75 g/3 oz pot barley

1.2 litres/2 pints Vegetable Stock (see page 11)

2 tablespoons malt extract

2 tablespoons chopped sage

100 g/3½ oz frozen peas, cooked and drained

chopped parsley, to garnish

salt and pepper

DUMPLINGS

125 g/4 oz self-raising flour

50 g/2 oz vegetable suet

2 tablespoons chopped parsley

4–5 tablespoons cold water

Heat the oil in a large flameproof casserole, add the onion and fry, stirring occasionally, for 4–5 minutes until lightly browned.

Add the carrots, parsnip, swede, barley, 900 m/1½ pints of the stock, the malt extract and sage. Bring to the boil. Cover and cook in a preheated oven, 180°C (350°F), Gas Mark 4, for 1 hour. Set aside.

Shortly before serving, make the dumplings. Mix the flour, suet and parsley in a bowl with a little salt and pepper. Add enough water to mix to a soft, slightly sticky dough. With floured hands, gently roll the mixture into 12 small balls.

Add the remaining stock to the stew and bring to the boil on the hob. Season lightly with salt and pepper if required, add the dumplings and replace the lid. Simmer on the hob for 10–12 minutes until the dumplings are well risen and fluffy, then sprinkle in the peas. Serve the stew in bowls, topped with a little chopped parsley.

chestnut sofrito

This aromatic casserole of chickpeas, chestnuts, carrots and sweet potato has a Middle Eastern flavour.

SERVES 2–3

1 tablespoon olive oil

1 onion, finely chopped

2 garlic cloves, crushed

2.5 cm/1 inch piece of fresh root ginger, peeled and finely chopped

1 sweet potato, about 200 g/7 oz, halved lengthways and thickly sliced

2 carrots, about 200 g/7 oz, diced

410 g/13½ oz can chopped tomatoes

450 ml/¾ pint Vegetable Stock (see page 11)

250 g/8 oz can whole chestnuts, drained

410 g/13½ oz can chickpeas, drained and rinsed

½ teaspoon turmeric

1 cinnamon stick, halved

salt and pepper

TO SERVE

175 g/6 oz couscous

450 ml/¾ pint boiling water

juice of 1 orange

4 tablespoons chopped mixed parsley and mint

Heat the oil in a casserole, add the onion and fry for 5 minutes until softened and pale golden. Stir in the garlic and ginger and cook for 2 minutes.

Add the sweet potato, carrots, tomatoes and stock to the casserole with the chestnuts and chickpeas and bring to the boil, stirring. Add the turmeric and cinnamon and season with salt and pepper. Cover the casserole and cook in a preheated oven, 180°C (350°F), Gas Mark 4, for 1 hour until tender.

Shortly before serving, put the couscous into a bowl, pour on the boiling water and leave to soak for 5 minutes. Drain any excess water from the couscous and stir in the orange juice, using a fork.

Stir the parsley and mint into the couscous and season with salt and pepper to taste. Spoon on to warm plates and top with sofrito.

quick thai vegetable curry

You can buy Thai basil leaves in Asian supermarkets. Kaffir lime leaves are available in most big supermarkets.

SERVES 4

2 tablespoons sunflower oil

1 onion, chopped

2 garlic cloves, crushed

5 cm/2 inch piece of fresh root ginger, peeled and grated

1½ tablespoons Thai red curry paste

600 ml/1 pint Vegetable Stock (see page 11)

3 kaffir lime leaves

250 g/8 oz sweet potatoes, peeled and diced

250 g/8 oz pumpkin, peeled, deseeded and cubed

8 baby sweetcorn cobs, trimmed

1 aubergine, roughly chopped

125 g/4 oz green beans, chopped

125 g/4 oz small button mushrooms

200 g/7 oz can bamboo shoots, drained

salt and pepper

plain boiled jasmine or brown rice, to serve

TO GARNISH

1 tablespoon grated fresh coconut

handful of Thai basil leaves

Heat the oil in a large saucepan, add the onion, garlic and ginger and fry gently for 5 minutes, stirring occasionally. Stir in the Thai red curry paste and fry gently for 3 minutes, stirring constantly.

Add the stock and kaffir lime leaves and bring to the boil; add salt and pepper to taste, then lower the heat and simmer for 2 minutes. Add the sweet potatoes and pumpkin, cover the pan and simmer for 10 minutes.

Stir in the sweetcorn, aubergine, green beans, mushrooms and bamboo shoots, replace the lid and simmer for a further 5–10 minutes, or until the beans are just tender but still crisp.

Taste and adjust the seasoning. Put the curry into a warmed serving dish and sprinkle with the coconut and basil leaves. Serve with rice.

roasted vegetables

Serve this as a healthy starter or, alternatively, you could serve the vegetables as a main course, with some steamed couscous.

SERVES 8

1 small butternut squash
2 beetroot
1 potato
½ cassava
2 carrots
2 red onions
1 courgette
125 ml/4 fl oz avocado oil
1 tablespoon soy sauce
4 whole garlic cloves
1 dessertspoon rosemary leaves
1 dessertspoon chopped fennel fronds
salt and pepper

TO SERVE
selection of dips
warm bread

Trim all the vegetables, then cut them into finger-sized pieces.

Put the avocado oil and soy sauce into a large bowl and mix well. Dip the vegetable pieces and garlic in and coat them well.

Arrange the squash, beetroot, potato and cassava pieces on a baking sheet and bake in a preheated oven, 180°C (350°F), Gas Mark 4, for 20 minutes.

Turn these vegetables over, then add the carrots, onions, courgette and garlic. Sprinkle with the rosemary and fennel, season with salt and pepper, then return the baking sheet to the oven for 25–30 minutes.

Serve with a selection of dips, such as hummus or sweet chilli sauce, and some warm bread.

navarin of spring vegetables

This is a delicious mixture of tender young vegetables in a buttery lemon broth, which enhances the flavours.

SERVES 4

250 g/8 oz small broad beans, defrosted
    if frozen

175 g/6 oz sugar snap peas, trimmed

175 g/6 oz fine young asparagus, trimmed
    and cut into 2.5 cm/1 inch pieces

75 g/3 oz butter

8 spring onions, sliced

2 garlic cloves, chopped

900 ml/1½ pints Chicken Stock or
    Vegetable Stock (see pages 10 and 11)

1 thyme sprig

15 baby onions, peeled

10 baby turnips or 3 small turnips,
    cut into wedges

250 g/8 oz small carrots

1½ tablespoons fresh lemon juice

salt and pepper

chopped chervil, to garnish

Blanch the broad beans, if using fresh ones, the sugar snap peas and asparagus in salted boiling water and refresh immediately in cold water. Drain and set aside. Pop the broad beans out of their skins.

Melt the butter in a large flameproof casserole over a low heat, add the spring onions and garlic and cook, without colouring, until softened. Add the stock and thyme and bring to the boil, then add the baby onions. Cover the casserole and simmer for 5 minutes.

Add the turnips, bring back to the boil, then reduce the heat and simmer for 6–8 minutes. Add the carrots and cook for 5–6 minutes. Season with salt, pepper and lemon juice. Add the beans, peas and asparagus and heat through. Serve garnished with the chervil.

vegetable and lentil hotchpotch

This budget-priced soup is a good way to use up the oddments from the vegetable rack and is tasty without being too spicy.

SERVES 4

1 tablespoon sunflower oil

1 onion, finely chopped

15 g/½ oz butter

2 carrots, about 250 g/8 oz, diced

1 potato, about 250 g/8 oz, diced

1 parsnip, about 250 g/8 oz, diced

½ teaspoon turmeric

3 teaspoons mild curry paste

1.2 litres/2 pints Vegetable Stock or
   Chicken Stock (see pages 11 and 10)

75 g/3 oz red lentils, rinsed

salt and pepper

chopped parsley, to garnish

crusty bread, to serve

Heat the oil in a saucepan, add the onion and fry for 5 minutes, stirring until softened. Add the butter and the diced carrots, potato and parsnip and fry for a further 5 minutes, stirring.

Stir in the turmeric and curry paste and cook for 1 minute, then add the stock and lentils and season with salt and pepper. Bring to the boil, then cover the pan and simmer very gently for 40 minutes until the lentils are soft. Ladle into bowls, sprinkle with a little parsley and serve with crusty bread.

FOOD **FACT**
A vegetarian staple, lentils do not require soaking before they can be used in a recipe. There are a number of varieties but the most commonly used are red and green lentils.

deep-fried tofu
with stir-fried vegetables

You want the vegetables to be cooked but to still retain some bite in a stir-fry,
so be careful not to overcook them.

SERVES 4

2 tablespoons sunflower oil

1 garlic clove, sliced

250 g/8 oz broccoli, cut into florets

125 g/4 oz green beans, halved

2 carrots, thinly sliced

150 ml/¼ pint hot Vegetable Stock
(see page 11)

3 tablespoons oyster sauce

2 tablespoons brown sugar

2 tablespoons sweet chilli sauce

250 g/8 oz ready-cooked firm tofu,
cut into cubes

125 g/4 oz bean sprouts

2 tablespoons chopped mint

boiled rice, to serve

Heat the sunflower oil in a wok and fry the garlic for 1 minute.
Remove with a slotted spoon and discard. Add the broccoli, beans and
carrots and stir-fry for 3 minutes.

Combine the stock, oyster sauce, sugar and chilli sauce in a jug and
pour into the wok. Add the tofu and cook for 2–3 minutes, until the tofu
is hot and the vegetables are tender. Stir in the bean sprouts and mint and
serve with boiled rice.

FOOD **FACT**
Tofu is a widely used meat alternative and an Asian staple that's available
in various forms. It's very versatile and, although it doesn't have a lot of
taste on its own, it will absorb the other flavours of the dish, so can be
used in many different kinds of recipes.

fennel and corn succotash

Succotash is a traditional native American vegetable stew. The key ingredients are sweetcorn and lima beans, although other beans can also be used.

SERVES 4

250 g/8 oz dried lima or flageolet beans, soaked overnight

75 g/3 oz butter

3 garlic cloves, crushed

2 shallots or 1 small onion, finely chopped

2 small fennel bulbs, finely sliced

1 red pepper, cored, deseeded and chopped

3 fresh sweetcorn cobs, husk and inner silks removed, cut into 2.5 cm/1 inch rounds, or 200 g/7 oz sweetcorn kernels, canned or frozen, defrosted if frozen

750 ml/1¼ pints Chicken Stock or Vegetable Stock (see pages 10 and 11)

2 tablespoons sherry or white wine vinegar

salt and pepper

Drain the beans, rinse well and place in a large saucepan with water to cover. Bring to the boil, then reduce the heat. Cover the pan and simmer for 45–60 minutes, or until the beans are tender. Drain and set aside.

Melt the butter in a large heavy-based saucepan, add the garlic and shallots or onion and cook for 5 minutes until lightly browned. Add the fennel and red pepper and cook for 15–20 minutes until softened.

Add the sweetcorn, if using fresh, and the stock and season to taste with salt and pepper. Bring to the boil, then reduce the heat, cover the pan and simmer for 20–30 minutes until the corn is tender. Remove the lid, add the drained beans, the canned or frozen corn, if using, and the sherry or vinegar.

Bring the succotash back to the boil and cook for about 5 minutes until the liquid has reduced and thickened slightly. Adjust the seasoning to taste and serve.

vegetable curry

Serve this on its own or as part of an Indian meal, with other curries and naan bread. Grated cucumber mixed with natural yogurt is a popular side dish.

SERVES 4

1 tablespoon olive oil

1 onion, chopped

1 garlic clove, crushed

2 tablespoons medium curry paste

1½ kg/3 lb prepared mixed vegetables (such as courgettes, peppers, squash, mushrooms and green beans)

200 g/7 oz can chopped tomatoes

410 g/13½ oz can coconut milk

2 tablespoons chopped coriander leaves

boiled rice, to serve

Heat the oil in a large saucepan, add the onion and garlic and fry for 2 minutes. Stir in the curry paste and fry for 1 minute more.

Add the vegetables and fry for 2–3 minutes, stirring occasionally, then add the tomatoes and coconut milk. Stir well and bring to the boil, then lower the heat and simmer for 12–15 minutes until all the vegetables are cooked. Stir in the chopped coriander and serve with rice.

FOOD **FACT**
Fresh coriander is a wonderfully fragrant herb that is used in many Indian dishes, as a main ingredient and also as a garnish. It's quite a delicate plant and won't keep very long so it's best to use it as fresh as possible or freeze any that's left in freezer bags, for future use.

beetroot risotto

This is a really colourful dish, thanks to the beetroot. If possible, try to cook raw beetroot, as the flavour will be better than bought varieties.

SERVES 4

1 tablespoon olive oil

15 g/½ oz butter

1 teaspoon crushed or coarsely ground coriander seeds

4 spring onions, thinly sliced

400 g/13 oz freshly cooked beetroot, cut into 1 cm/½ inch dice

500 g/1 lb arborio or other risotto rice

1.5 litres/2½ pints hot Vegetable Stock (see page 11)

200 g/7 oz cream cheese

4 tablespoons finely chopped dill

salt and pepper

TO GARNISH

dill sprigs

crème fraîche

Heat the oil and butter in a large shallow heavy-based saucepan. Add the crushed coriander seeds and spring onions and stir-fry briskly for 1 minute.

Add the beetroot and the rice. Cook, stirring, for 2–3 minutes to coat all the grains with the oil and butter. Gradually pour in the hot stock, a ladleful at a time, stirring often until each ladleful is absorbed before adding the next. This should take about 20 minutes, by which time the rice should be *al dente*, tender, but still firm to the bite.

Stir in the cream cheese and dill, and season to taste with salt and pepper. Serve immediately in bowls, garnished with dill sprigs and a little crème fraîche.

pumpkin and pine nut risotto

Pine nuts are used extensively in Italian cookery, in both savoury and sweet dishes. They have a lovely buttery taste and texture.

SERVES 4–5

500 g/1 lb pumpkin, deseeded
45 g/1½ oz butter
2 tablespoons olive oil
50 g/2 oz pine nuts
1 onion, chopped
2 garlic cloves, crushed
275 g/9 oz arborio or other risotto rice
150 ml/¼ pint white wine
900 ml/1½ pints hot Chicken Stock or
    Vegetable Stock (see pages 10 and 11)
40 g/1½ oz freshly grated Parmesan
    cheese
salt and pepper

Cut away the skin from the pumpkin and cut the flesh into 1.5 cm/ ¾ inch chunks. Melt half the butter in a large heavy-based saucepan with the oil and fry the pumpkin for 3 minutes. Add the pine nuts and cook for 2 minutes until pale golden. Remove the pumpkin chunks and pine nuts with a slotted spoon and set aside.

Add the onion to the pan and fry for 3–4 minutes until very soft. Add the garlic and rice and cook, stirring, for 1 minute. Pour in the wine and let it bubble until it has evaporated.

Add a little of the hot stock and cook, stirring, until it is absorbed. Add a little more stock and cook until absorbed. Continue cooking, gradually adding all the remaining stock, for about 20 minutes, stirring until the risotto is thick and creamy but the grains retain a little texture. You might not need all the stock.

Return the pumpkin and the pine nuts to the pan with the remaining butter and half the Parmesan. Check the seasoning and spoon the risotto on to warm plates. Sprinkle with the remaining Parmesan.

chicken, pea and mint risotto

Risotto cooked in the oven is not usually as creamy as a risotto stirred over the hob, so this recipe includes a little cream to add at the end to compensate for it.

SERVES 4

25 g/1 oz butter

1 onion, finely chopped

150 g/5 oz skinless chicken breast fillet, cut into strips

200 g/7 oz arborio or other risotto rice

1 teaspoon fennel seeds

900 ml/1½ pints hot Chicken Stock (see page 10)

75 g/3 oz frozen peas, thawed

juice and grated rind of 1 lemon

2 tablespoons double cream

100 g/3½ oz Parmesan cheese, freshly grated

2 tablespoons chopped mint

salt and pepper

Heat the butter in a large flameproof casserole and fry the onion and chicken for 3 minutes. Add the rice and fennel seeds and stir for 30 seconds, then add the stock and peas. Cover tightly and cook in a preheated oven, 200°C (400°F), Gas Mark 6, for 20 minutes until the rice is tender and all the liquid has been absorbed.

Stir in the lemon juice and rind, double cream and Parmesan and season with salt and pepper. Cover and leave for 2 minutes, then stir in the mint. Serve immediately.

boston baked beans

Real home-made baked beans are a revelation. Serve on toast for a light meal,
or as an accompaniment to sausages or grilled meat.

SERVES 2

1 tablespoon vegetable oil

1 small red onion, finely chopped

2 celery sticks, finely chopped

1 garlic clove, crushed

200 g/7 oz can chopped tomatoes

150 ml/¼ pint Vegetable Stock
(see page 11)

1 tablespoon dark soy sauce

1 tablespoon dark brown sugar

2 teaspoons Dijon mustard

410 g/13½ oz can mixed beans,
drained and rinsed

2 tablespoons chopped parsley

Heat the oil in a heavy-based saucepan. Add the onion and cook over
a low heat for 5 minutes, or until softened. Add the celery and garlic and
continue to cook for 1–2 minutes.

Add the tomatoes, stock and soy sauce. Bring to the boil, then reduce
the heat to a fast simmer and cook for about 15 minutes, or until the
sauce begins to thicken.

Add the sugar, mustard and beans. Continue to cook for a further
5 minutes, or until the beans are heated through. Stir in the chopped
parsley and serve.

FOOD **FACT**
Celery is often only used raw in salads or eaten with cheese and biscuits
but in fact it's delicious cooked and can impart a wonderful flavour to
dishes. It is also low in calories.

chicken and lemon paella

Chicken and lemon make a classic flavour combination and they're combined with other colourful ingredients in this delicious paella.

SERVES 2

4 teaspoons olive oil

300 g/10 oz boneless, skinless chicken thighs, diced

1 onion, sliced

2 garlic cloves, crushed

1 red pepper, cored, deseeded and roughly chopped

75 g/3 oz easy-cook white long-grain rice

2 tablespoons dry sherry

250 ml/8 fl oz Chicken Stock (see page 10)

200 g/7 oz frozen peas

grated rind and juice of 1 lemon

salt and pepper

thyme sprigs, to garnish

lemon wedges, to serve

Heat 2 teaspoons of the oil in a frying pan over a medium heat and cook the chicken for 4–6 minutes, or until golden. Remove from the pan and add the remaining oil. Add the onion and cook over a medium heat for 10 minutes until soft. Add the garlic and red pepper and cook for 3 minutes.

Stir in the rice and pour in the sherry and stock. Return the chicken to the pan. Turn the heat to low and cook for 10–15 minutes.

Add the peas and cook for a further 2–3 minutes, or until the liquid has evaporated. Stir in the lemon rind and juice, then season to taste with salt and pepper. Serve garnished with thyme sprigs and accompanied by lemon wedges.

FOOD **FACT**
Made in Spain, sherry is the obvious ingredient to include in this paella dish. The alcohol will mainly burn off during cooking, so you'll be left with all the rich flavours of the sherry, which will add a twist to this classic.

red beans with coconut
and cashews

The cashew nuts add a delicious crunch to this bean stew. Make sure that you buy the unsalted variety.

SERVES 4

3 tablespoons vegetable oil

2 onions, chopped

2 small carrots, thinly sliced

3 garlic cloves, crushed

1 red pepper, cored, deseeded and chopped

2 bay leaves

1 tablespoon paprika

3 tablespoons tomato purée

400 ml/14 fl oz can coconut milk

200 g/7 oz can chopped tomatoes

150 ml/¼ pint Vegetable Stock (see page 11)

410 g/13½ oz can red kidney beans, rinsed and drained

100 g/3½ oz unsalted, shelled cashew nuts, toasted

small handful of coriander leaves, roughly chopped

rice, to serve

Heat the oil in a large saucepan. Add the onions and carrots and fry for 3 minutes. Add the garlic, red pepper and bay leaves and fry for 5 minutes or until the vegetables are soft and well browned.

Stir in the paprika, tomato purée, coconut milk, tomatoes, stock and beans and bring to the boil. Reduce the heat and simmer, uncovered, for about 12 minutes, or until the vegetables are tender.

Add the cashew nuts and coriander and heat through for 2 minutes. Serve the beans with rice.

black beans and rice
cooked in stout

Historically, stout used to be used a lot in cooking, probably as it was often safer to drink than the water. That isn't the case now, but that's no reason to omit it!

SERVES 6

1 teaspoon cumin seeds

1 teaspoon coriander seeds

500 g/1 lb dried black beans, soaked overnight

3 tablespoons olive oil

2 onions, chopped

3 garlic cloves, crushed

1 green chilli, deseeded and finely chopped

½ teaspoon chilli powder

2 teaspoons thyme leaves

2 bay leaves

2 tablespoons black treacle

500 g/1 lb tomatoes, skinned and chopped

300 ml/½ pint stout

1 litre/1¾ pints water

175 g/6 oz long-grain rice

4 tablespoons chopped coriander leaves

salt and pepper

SALSA

4 spring onions, finely sliced

1 garlic clove, chopped

4 tomatoes, chopped

1 tablespoon chopped coriander leaves

75 g/3 oz canned sweetcorn kernels, drained

2 tablespoons fresh lime juice

Put the cumin and coriander seeds into a dry frying pan over a medium heat and cook, stirring, for 1–2 minutes until fragrant; do not let them burn. Leave to cool, then grind to a powder in a spice grinder or use a pestle and mortar. Drain the beans and rinse well.

Heat the oil in a large flameproof casserole, add the onions, garlic, green chilli, chilli powder and thyme and cook for 6–8 minutes until softened. Add all the remaining ingredients, except the rice and coriander. Bring to the boil, then reduce the heat, cover the pan and simmer over a very low heat for 1½–2 hours. Check occasionally and top up with boiling water if the mixture seems dry.

Add the rice and season with salt and pepper, cover the casserole and cook for 30 minutes, or until the beans and rice are very tender. Remove the casserole from the heat, stir in the chopped coriander, cover, and leave for 5 minutes.

To prepare the salsa, mix together all the ingredients in a bowl and serve with the beans and rice.

campfire bean pot

This might be a little too sophisticated for most campfires but it's perfect for enjoying at home with a group of friends.

SERVES 4–6

500 g/1 lb dried haricot beans, soaked overnight

25 g/1 oz soft brown sugar

¼ teaspoon ground cinnamon

2 teaspoons mustard powder

4 tablespoons molasses or black treacle

1 large onion, chopped

2 garlic cloves, crushed

4 tomatoes, skinned and chopped

1 thyme sprig

1 bay leaf

2 cloves

375 g/12 oz piece of belly of pork, scored, or rindless streaky bacon

50–75 ml/2–3 fl oz dark rum (optional)

salt and pepper

sweetcorn cobs and sausages, to serve

Drain the beans, rinse well and place in a large flameproof casserole. In a small bowl, mix together the sugar, cinnamon, mustard and molasses or treacle, then add to the beans. Add all the remaining ingredients, except the rum, pushing the pork, or streaky bacon down into the centre of the beans.

Pour over water to cover, about 600 ml/1 pint, bring to the boil, then cover the casserole with a tight-fitting lid and bake in a preheated oven, 150°C (300°F), Gas Mark 2, for 3–4 hours. Check occasionally and top up with boiling water, if the mixture seems too dry.

Stir in the rum, if using, and adjust the seasoning to taste. Remove the pork or bacon, slice it and place the slices on top of the casserole. Return the casserole to the oven and cook, uncovered, for 20–30 minutes. Serve with sweetcorn cobs and sausages.

FOOD **FACT**
Molasses is made from sugarcane juices that are unprocessed. It has a thick, syrupy consistency and is a popular ingredient for baking, especially in America.

italian lamb and broad beans

The wild mushrooms make this a really special dish – try to buy a nice selection of different varieties.

SERVES 4

2 tablespoons olive oil

500 g/1 lb lean boneless leg of lamb, trimmed and cut into 2.5 cm/1 inch cubes

410 g/13½ oz can tomatoes

150 ml/¼ pint water

1 rosemary sprig

1 thyme sprig

1 bay leaf

125 g/4 oz mixed wild mushrooms, roughly chopped

75 g/3 oz frozen broad beans

salt and pepper

chopped flat leaf parsley, to garnish

Heat the oil in a flameproof casserole. Add the lamb and cook, stirring frequently, for 5 minutes, or until evenly browned. Stir in the tomatoes with their juice and the water. Add the rosemary, thyme and bay leaf and season with salt and pepper to taste. Stir well, then cover the casserole and simmer for 45 minutes.

Add the chopped mushrooms and broad beans to the casserole. Taste for seasoning. Cover the casserole and simmer gently for a further 20 minutes.

Discard the rosemary, thyme and bay leaf and serve sprinkled with chopped parsley.

FOOD **FACT**
Broad beans are a popular vegetable for growing in the garden as they grow quickly and are quite easy to maintain. They're also delicious in salads and soups and are a popular addition to many Italian recipes.

beef and bean stew
with cornmeal dumplings

These tasty dumplings are well worth making and their addition makes this stew a meal in itself.

SERVES 4–6

375 g/12 oz dried red or black kidney beans, soaked overnight

2 tablespoons olive oil

750 g/1½ lb boneless shin of beef, cut into 2.5 cm/1 inch cubes

1 large onion, chopped

2–3 garlic cloves, crushed

2 teaspoons ground cumin

2 teaspoons ground coriander

2–3 large fresh red chillies, roasted, peeled, deseeded and finely chopped

2 red peppers, roasted, peeled, deseeded and finely chopped

1 bay leaf

1 thyme sprig

2 large tomatoes, about 300 g/10 oz, skinned and chopped

600 ml/1 pint Beef Stock (see page 12)

6 tablespoons chopped coriander leaves

salt

CORNMEAL DUMPLINGS

65 g/2½ oz plain flour

75 g/3 oz fine cornmeal

1½ teaspoons caster sugar

1 teaspoon baking powder

¼ teaspoon salt

100 ml/3½ fl oz buttermilk, at room temperature

1 egg, beaten

25 g/1 oz unsalted butter, melted

50 g/2 oz canned sweetcorn kernels, drained

Drain the beans and rinse well. Heat the oil in a large flameproof casserole, add the meat in batches and brown well all over. Remove the meat with a slotted spoon and set aside.

Add the onion and garlic to the casserole and cook until the onion is golden brown, then add the cumin and coriander and cook for 1–2 minutes.

Add the drained beans, the meat and all the remaining ingredients, except the fresh coriander and salt, and just enough water to cover, about 300 ml/½ pint. Bring to the boil, then reduce the heat, cover the casserole tightly and simmer for 2–2½ hours until the meat is tender.

To make the dumplings, sift together the flour, cornmeal, sugar, baking powder and salt. Add the buttermilk, egg and butter and stir until combined, then gently stir in the sweetcorn.

Stir the coriander leaves into the stew and season with salt. Drop 12 spoonfuls of the dumpling mixture over the stew, replace the lid and cook for 10–15 minutes until the dumplings are light and cooked. Serve hot.

index

A

apple, borscht with 64
apricots: Moroccan lamb 88
  saffron chicken with apricots 74
aubergines: lamb and aubergine casserole 28
  lamb with aubergines 86
  Mediterranean stew 101

B

barley: vegetable and barley stew 108
beans: beef and bean stew 139
  black bean and cabbage stew 110
  black beans and rice cooked in stout 134
  Boston baked beans 130
  campfire bean pot 135
  chilli con carne 140
  chunky chilli bean and carrot soup 52
  chunky chorizo, pasta and bean soup 70
  clam, potato and bean stew 46
  fennel and corn succotash 120
  minestrone verde with red pesto 63
  pumpkin and root vegetable stew 118
  red beans with coconut and cashews 132
  sausage and bean casserole 41
  spicy sausage cassoulet 38
beef: beef and bean stew 139
  beef and prune casserole 44
  beef and pumpkin curry 94
  beef tagine 96
  Catalan beef stew with chocolate 92
  chilli con carne 140
  daube of beef 42

Middle Eastern beef casserole 93
  one-pot beef 45
  stock 12
beetroot: beetroot risotto 124
  borscht with apple 64
biryani, chicken 80
black beans: black bean and cabbage stew 110
  black beans and rice cooked in stout 134
black-eyed beans: spicy sausage cassoulet 38
borlotti beans: chunky chorizo, pasta and bean soup 70
borscht with apple 64
Boston baked beans 130
bread: tomato and bread soup 62
broad beans, Italian lamb and 138
broccoli: quick pesto pea and broccoli soup 54
butternut squash: chicken with lemon and 20
  gingered butternut squash and sweet potato soup 55

C

cabbage: black bean and cabbage stew 110
Cambodian fish hotpot 48
campfire bean pot 135
cannellini beans: clam, potato and bean stew 46
carrots: chunky chilli bean and carrot soup 52
  Irish stew 31
  one pot pork roast 37
cashews, red beans with coconut and 132
cassoulet, spicy sausage 38
Catalan beef stew with chocolate 92
cheese: beetroot risotto 124
  French onion soup 56

chestnuts: braised pheasant with Marsala and 24
  chestnut sofrito 109
chicken: chicken and lemon paella 131
  chicken and spinach masala 83
  chicken biryani 80
  chicken cacciatore 77
  chicken, lemon and olive stew 78
  chicken, pea and mint risotto 129
  chicken with coriander, saffron and almonds 16
  chicken with lemon and butternut squash 20
  chicken with lemon and olives 18
  coq au vin 84
  easy one-pot chicken 19
  harira 65
  Moroccan red chicken 76
  saffron chicken with apricots 74
  stock 10
  Thai chicken curry 82
chickpeas: beef tagine 96
  chestnut sofrito 109
  easy lamb tagine 87
  harira 65
  lamb soup with couscous and 66
  Middle Eastern beef casserole 93
  Moroccan lamb 88
  Moroccan pumpkin and lamb couscous 136
chillies: beef and bean stew 139
  Cambodian fish hotpot 48
  chilli con carne 140
  chunky chilli bean and carrot soup 52
chocolate, Catalan beef stew with 92
chorizo, pasta and bean soup 70

clams: Cambodian fish hotpot 48
  clam, potato and bean stew 46
  pork and clam stew 35
coconut: Cambodian fish hotpot 48
  red beans with cashews and 132
  sweet potato and coconut soup 59
coq au vin 84
coriander: vegetable curry 121
corn: fennel and corn succotash 120
cornmeal dumplings 139
courgettes: Middle Eastern beef casserole 93
couscous: lamb soup with chickpeas and 66
  Moroccan pumpkin and lamb couscous 136
  North African fish stew 100
cumin: Moroccan red chicken 76
curries: beef and pumpkin curry 94
  chicken and spinach masala 83
  creamy prawn curry 102
  quick Thai vegetable curry 112
  Thai chicken curry 82
  Thai monkfish and prawn curry 98
  vegetable curry 121

D

daube of beef 42
duck: roasted duck with spiced lentils 22
  spicy duck in port with fresh figs 23
dumplings 108, 139

E

equipment 8

F
fennel and corn succotash 120
figs, spicy duck in port with 23
fish: Cambodian fish hotpot 48
   Moroccan fish soup 68
   North African fish stew 100
   stock 13
   see also individual types of
      fish
French onion soup 56

G
gingered butternut squash and
   sweet potato soup 55
goulash, pumpkin 106

H
haricot beans: campfire bean
   pot 135
   minestrone verde with red
      pesto 63
harira 65
herbs 9
hunter-style rabbit stew 25

I
ingredients 8–9
Irish stew 31
Italian lamb and broad beans
   138

L
lamb: easy lamb tagine 87
   Irish stew 31
   Italian lamb and broad beans
      138
   lamb and aubergine casserole
      28
   lamb and lentil hotpot 30
   lamb balti 90
   lamb shanks with olives 26
   lamb soup with chickpeas and
      couscous 66
   lamb with aubergines 86
   lamb with garlic, lemon and
      mint 29
   Mediterranean stew 101
   Moroccan lamb 88
   Moroccan pumpkin and lamb
      couscous 136
lemon grass: Thai chicken curry
   82
lentils: lamb and lentil hotpot 30

pumpkin goulash 106
roasted duck with spiced
   lentils 22
sausages with lentils 40
spicy lentil and tomato soup
   58
vegetable and lentil
   hotchpotch 116
lima beans: fennel and corn
   succotash 120

M
Mediterranean stew 101
Middle Eastern beef casserole
   93
minestrone verde with red pesto
   63
molasses: campfire bean pot
   135
monkfish and prawn curry, Thai
   98
Moroccan fish soup 68
Moroccan lamb 88
Moroccan pumpkin and lamb
   couscous 136
Moroccan red chicken 76
mushrooms: Cambodian fish
   hotpot 48
   chicken cacciatore 77
   coq au vin 84
   lamb and lentil hotpot 30

N
navarin of spring vegetables
   115
North African fish stew 100

O
olive oil 9
olives 9
   chicken, lemon and olive stew
      78
   chicken with lemon and olives
      18
   daube of beef 42
   lamb shanks with olives 26
onions: coq au vin 84
   French onion soup 56
   lamb with aubergines 86
osso buco, orange 97

P
paella, chicken and lemon 131

pancetta: sausages with lentils
   40
paprika pork 34
parsnips: one pot pork roast 37
pasta: chunky chorizo, pasta
   and bean soup 70
peas: chicken and lemon paella
   131
   chicken, pea and mint risotto
      129
   quick pesto pea and broccoli
      soup 54
peppers: beef and bean stew
   139
   bright red pepper soup 60
   peppered pork 36
   pork and clam stew 35
   sausage and bean casserole
      41
   Thai chicken curry 82
pesto: minestrone verde with red
   pesto 63
   quick pesto pea and broccoli
      soup 54
pheasant with Marsala and
   chestnuts 24
pine nuts: pumpkin and pine nut
   risotto 128
pork: campfire bean pot 135
   one pot pork roast 37
   paprika pork 34
   peppered pork 36
   pork and clam stew 35
   pot roast pork with juniper and
      rosemary 32
potatoes: black bean and
   cabbage stew 110
   clam, potato and bean stew
      46
   Irish stew 31
   lamb and aubergine casserole
      with a potato crust 28
   lamb and lentil hotpot 30
   lamb balti 90
   one-pot beef 45
   one pot pork roast 37
prawns: Cambodian fish hotpot
   48
   creamy prawn curry 102
   Thai monkfish and prawn
      curry 98
prunes: beef and prune
   casserole 44

sausages with lentils 40
pumpkin: beef and pumpkin
   curry 94
   Moroccan pumpkin and lamb
      couscous 136
   pumpkin and pine nut risotto
      128
   pumpkin and root vegetable
      stew 118
   pumpkin goulash 106

R
rabbit stew, hunter-style 25
red cabbage: roasted duck with
   spiced lentils 22
red kidney beans: beef and bean
   stew 139
   chilli con carne 140
   chunky chilli bean and carrot
      soup 52
   pumpkin and root vegetable
      stew 118
   red beans with coconut and
      cashews 132
rice: beetroot risotto 124
   black beans and rice cooked
      in stout 134
   chicken and lemon paella 131
   chicken biryani 80
   chicken, pea and mint risotto
      129
   green vegetable risotto 126
   pumpkin and pine nut risotto
      128

S
saffron chicken with apricots 74
sausages: chunky chorizo, pasta
   and bean soup 70
   sausage and bean casserole
      41
   sausages with lentils 40
   spicy sausage cassoulet 38
smoked haddock: creamy
   haddock and spinach
   chowder 69
soups 51–71, 116
spices 9
spinach: chicken and spinach
   masala 83
   creamy haddock and spinach
      chowder 69
squash *see* butternut squash

squid: Cambodian fish hotpot 48
stock 8, 10–13
succotash, fennel and corn 120
sweet potatoes: gingered
    butternut squash and sweet
    potato soup 55
  sweet potato and coconut
    soup 59
sweetcorn: fennel and corn
    succotash 120

T
tagines 87, 96
Thai chicken curry 82
Thai monkfish and prawn curry
  98
tofu: deep-fried tofu with stir-
    fried vegetables 117
tomatoes: black beans and rice

cooked in stout 134
Boston baked beans 130
chicken cacciatore 77
chilli con carne 140
chunky chilli bean and carrot
    soup 52
hunter-style rabbit stew 25
lamb and aubergine casserole
    with a potato crust 28
Mediterranean stew 101
sausage and bean casserole
    41
spicy lentil and tomato soup
    58
tomato and bread soup 62

V
veal: orange osso buco 97
vegetables 9

beef tagine 96
chestnut sofrito 109
deep-fried tofu with stir-fried
    vegetables 117
easy one-pot chicken 19
green vegetable risotto 126
minestrone verde with red
    pesto 63
navarin of spring vegetables
    115
one-pot beef 45
pumpkin and root vegetable
    stew 118
quick Thai vegetable curry
    112
roasted vegetables 114
stock 11
vegetable and lentil
    hotchpotch 116

vegetable curry 121
vegetables and barley stew
  108
see also individual types of
  vegetable

W
wine: chicken cacciatore 77
  coq au vin 84
  daube of beef 42
  hunter-style rabbit stew 25

acknowledgements

Executive Editor Nicola Hill
Editor Charlotte Wilson
Executive Art Director Leigh Jones
Designer Lisa Tai
Senior Production Controller Manjit Sihra
Picture Researcher Jenifer Veall

picture acknowledgements

Octopus Publishing Group Limited/ Clive Bozzard-Hill 114 bottom right/ Stephen Conroy 13 bottom right, 95 main, 128 bottom left, 137 main/ Laurie Evans 7 top right/ David Jordan 5 top centre right, 22 bottom right, 50-51 main, 53 main, 69 bottom right, 91 main, 101 bottom right, 107 main/ Sandra Lane 9 top right, 9 bottom left/W. Adams Lingwood 8 top left/ William Lingwood 2 main, 5 top right, 5 bottom right, 14-15 main, 21 main, 39 main, 45 top left, 71 main, 89 main, 99 main, 129 bottom right, 141 main/ David Loftus 49 main, 68 top right, 75 main, 127 main/ Neil Mersh 5 centre right, 72-73 main, 81 main, 83 bottom right, 103 main, 125 main/ Peter Myers 5 bottom centre right, 17 main, 23 top left, 27 main, 29 bottom, 33 main, 34 bottom right, 35 bottom right, 44 bottom right, 100 bottom right, 104-105 main, 115 bottom right/Sean Myers 57 main, 85 main/ William Reavell 1 centre, 11 bottom right, 61 main, 111 main, 113 main, 122 main, 133 main/ Simon Smith 6 bottom left/ Ian Wallace 42 main, 47 main, 62 Bottom, 67 main, 79 main/ Philip Webb 119 main.